BUSINESS 101

WHILE YOU'RE DOING YOUR 1'S AND 2'S

Gina Calhoun

a result of the use of the information contained within this document. This includes, but is not limited to, errors, omissions, inaccuracies, or the fact that you actually tried one of these ideas and got fired. That means you did something wrong on your end, not the book's fault.

Basically, if your career implodes, your bank account hits zero, or your boss throws a stapler at you because of something you read here, that's on you, and you did not do a good job of learning from the book. The author is not a doctor, a lawyer, or a financial advisor; the author is just someone who wrote a book you're currently holding. Use your own damn brain.

ISBN: 979-8-9949938-0-4

Description: When most people think of a business book, two things come to mind:

1. "Cool, I'm going to learn something useful."
2. "Ugh… this is going to be boring as hell."

If you're like me, it's usually the second one.

I've spent my career in industries that were mostly male-dominated, and I've met two types of people:

- The ones who treat business books like the Bible.
- The ones who'd rather scroll TikTok, watching skateboard fails and golden retrievers doing laps in pools.

And honestly? I get it. Reading can feel like homework.

That's why **this book exists**.

This isn't your boring, jargon-filled, "must-take-notes" kind of business book. This is for people who hate business books. People who think, "If I wanted a lecture, I'd sit through a meeting that should've been an email."

This book is a bathroom-read, short-attention-span-friendly, laugh-out-loud guide to starting, running, and growing your business as an owner, manager, or employee. It covers marketing, sales, money hacks, reviews, and advice, all without putting you to sleep.

So, if you want a business book you might actually finish (and maybe even learn something from), welcome. You've finally found it.

DEDICATION

To my husband, Jason, and my sons, Justice and Taytum, thank you for fully accepting that your wife/mom is a certified weirdo who can go from "loving parent" to "feral raccoon with two cell phones" in 0.2 seconds but also broadcast to the world that, yes, you are related to me. You've stuck around through my half-assed business ideas, my motivational speeches that sound like TED Talks for lunatics, and my occasional "I'm running away to Mexico" meltdowns and still haven't fled the country. That's true love (or Stockholm Syndrome, but hey, it works).

To my family (blood-related or just stuck with me): Thanks for listening to all the complaining about the business. While some people think working 24/7 is insane, you never get mad when we miss your parties. You get it, we'd *much rather* be drinking, laughing, and dancing than powder coating signs until midnight. But hey, apparently this is what "building a future" looks like: smelling like chemicals, rocking raccoon eyes, and bragging about the smoothness of a finish like it's fine wine.

Thanks for not judging… too hard.

Mom: I listen, I promise… I just might occasionally, intentionally, and with full confidence ignore you on some things you say. Sorry… not sorry. I don't think I need a lot of sleep so we are good. Just know I love you to the moon and back.

Dad: Even though you're not around anymore, chillin with those angels, rum and coke in hand, I try my hardest not to swear. I know you're listening in Heaven. (Yes, Dad, I said try, not that I actually follow it.)

To you both: Thanks for teaching me how to bust my ass and work for what I get since I was 12. I'm finally ready for you to stop hiding those millions from me now.

Now to the assholes I call my employees, aka the beautiful disasters that make my workday feel like an episode of *The Office* but with more heavy machines, tools, and fewer HR complaints (barely).

- To the one who thinks being "5 minutes late" actually means 27, congrats, you've broken the space-time continuum.

- To the guy who always "forgets" where we keep the tools, buddy, you've worked here for years; the chemicals are in the chemical room, it didn't grow legs.

- To the genius who thought putting metal in the microwave was a good idea to see what would happen, thank you for ensuring I'll never forget the smell of melted stupidity.

- To the shop comedians 95% of your jokes suck, but that one about the difference between the fridge and butt that nearly made me pee my pants, so you get a pass.

- And to all of you collectively, you're the reason I say "I quit" at least once a day and then show up the next morning like nothing happened.

We've built this company, this chaos, this culture, and no matter how many times I fantasize about tossing one of you into the powder coating oven set to "extra crispy," (Don't worry, OSHA, if you're reading this, I didn't) I wouldn't trade you for anyone else. You're my dysfunctional second life line, and somehow, we make it work.

Seriously, though, you make the grind worth it, and the screw ups way more entertaining. You make work fun. You make me scream into a pillow, but like… in a loving way.

So here's to us: our chaos cluster, our ride-or-die crew, my insane people, my employees-who-should-probably-be-committed. Thanks for being part of this circus.

P.S. Jason, if this book sells big time, we're not just getting that coffee pot; I'm building a panic room.

TABLE OF CONTENTS

DON'T BE A RICHARD... OK FUCK IT... DON'T BE A DICK

(OWNER, MANAGER, OR EMPLOYEE, YES, YOU.)

Let's just get this out of the way: The world already has enough assholes. Don't add to the population.

This rule applies to everyone, but since this is a business book, we'll keep it focused on you. No matter your title, don't be a jerk. It's really that simple.

At our company, we spend more time with our coworkers than we do with our own families. So why the hell would you want to make that experience worse by bringing in a crap attitude? I've literally sent people home for showing up with bad vibes. Why? Because a bad attitude spreads like cancer, it poisons the room fast.

Your workplace should be your safe zone. Got drama at home? Sorry, but no one at work signed up for it. Leave it at the door. Don't show up like a walking rain cloud and expect others to just "deal with it."

Here's the truth: work doesn't have to suck. It can actually be fun. It should be filled with laughs, good energy, and people you (mostly) enjoy. But that doesn't happen if you drag in emotional garbage and dump it on everyone else.

OWNERS AND MANAGERS:

Your job is to lead, not to bark orders. Yes, sometimes you have to put on your "adult babysitter" hat; let's not pretend otherwise. But when you have employees who don't need to be micromanaged, do everyone a favor: leave them the hell alone. They've got it handled. Hovering over them just kills morale and slows things down. How would you like it if someone with probably 3-hour coffee breath was breathing down your neck all day? Exactly.. You would be right with them throwing a fit. Nowhere is it written in stone that work has to be miserable. There's a fine line between screwing off and actually enjoying being at work, and once you find that line, bend it, erase it, redraw it, whatever works. Do that, and suddenly you go home happier, you actually like your job again, and best of all, you might just avoid adding to the ever-growing dickhead population.

So again, just don't be a dick. It's amazing how far that one rule can take you in business and life. Decide to wake up in a good mood. It really isn't that hard unless you are a miserable person and you like pity parties. We all have things happen to us, and we are all going through something. Yes, it can be rough, but do not be a dick to others because of what is going on in your life. You want to let out those frustrations, go invest in one of those boxing bags and beat the shit out of that. You want to be an ass, just go hide in a hole because none of us need to deal with that.

CHAPTER 2

YOU'RE NOT ALWAYS RIGHT (SHOCKER, I KNOW)

If you think you're always right, congratulations, you're officially that person. You know, the one everyone rolls their eyes at the second you leave the room. You're not perfect. You're not a genius. You're just... human. Which means you're wrong sometimes, and there are people out there who know more than you and are smarter than you. (Yes, even you, Mr. CEO with the Customized Pen Set.)

Now, before employees start celebrating like they just won the lottery, let me say this: **you're not always right either.** Sorry, but asking your boss "why" 47 times a day isn't cute; it's exhausting. If your boss says, "Do it this way," your job isn't to launch an FBI-level interrogation. Just do it at least at first.

But, and this is a big but (insert bathroom joke here), if while you're doing it, your brain lights up with a faster, smarter, better way? **That's your moment**. That's when you say: "Hey, I know you asked me to do it this way, and I tried it, but I think I've got a method that saves time/money/sanity. Want to hear it?"

See the difference? That phrasing doesn't make your boss want to strangle you with a phone charger. It makes you look like you actually care.

Now, bosses, yes, I'm talking to you, Captain Clipboard, this is where you need to take a breath. Just because you've done something the same way since Blockbuster (if you are too young to know what Blockbuster is, then congratulations, you are in a lead role pretty young, so don't fuck it up). If your employee brings you a legit improvement, maybe (just maybe) shut your mouth for five seconds and listen. The next chapter will give you explanations of this magic world of WHYS.

The golden rule here? **Leaders: you're not always right. Employees: You're not always right either.** But together, you might actually stumble into something that works better than the old "because I said so" method.

So, the next time you're 100% certain you've got it all figured out, remember:

- You're human.

- You've been wrong before.

- You'll be wrong again.

- And that's okay unless you're still insisting MySpace is making a comeback. Then we need to talk, and I feel there can be a whole other book about how you need therapy at this point.

MYSPACE REVIVAL STRATEGY
– 0 LIKES
SALES
SALES
MAYBE WE'RE BOTH WRONG... AGAIN.
THIS IS HOW EMPIRES OR SUCCEED... PROBABLY CRUMBLE.
OOPS
OUR BRILLIANT PLAN
BECAUSE I SAID SO

TRUST FALL TIME:

(This is the time you go do an activity, and I trust you not to eff it up. I know you got this.)

We will start off easy. Go on your favorite social media platform and just have fun. You need a break from work sometimes.

SURVIVING THE GENERATION OF PERPETUAL 'WHY

I am assuming all of us know someone born in 1995 or later? Then you already know what this chapter is about. Every instruction comes with an immediate follow-up: "Why?" Do this report. Why? Come in at 9. Why? Wear pants. Why?"

By the end of the day, you're questioning your own existence, your career choices, and whether or not you should've just opened that alpaca farm in Montana like you dreamed.

And the kicker? Half the time their "Why?" actually makes sense, which is way more annoying. Suddenly, you're stuck explaining a process that was invented in 1998 by some manager named Carl who retired into obscurity with his bowling trophies. Spoiler: Carl's way isn't always the best way.

So buckle up, you're about to learn how to survive the generation that treats "Why?" like it's punctuation.

1. **They Don't Like Dumb Rules**

   If you tell them, "Do X because that's how we've always done it," don't be surprised when they respond with, "Yeah… but why?" They're not trying to be annoying; they just genuinely want to know if there's a reason behind your process. Old-school thinking: "Because I said so" doesn't cut it anymore.

2. **Efficiency Is Their Middle Name**

   Most of them grew up with smartphones that do their homework for them. If there's a smarter, faster, easier way to do something, they will find it. They ask "Why?" because they're thinking: "Can we do this better?" Not: "Can I ruin your day?"

3. **Curiosity Is In Their DNA**

   This generation has been spoon-fed information, tutorials, YouTube hacks, and Google answers since birth. Asking "Why?" is just their way of connecting the dots; they literally can't help it.

4. **They're Avoiding Meaningless Work**

   If they're doing something that seems pointless, they'll question it. And good on them, no one wants to work like a zombie pushing buttons for no reason. Sometimes their "Why?" is really, "I don't want to waste my life, and I like being efficient."

5. **They Might Actually Be Smarter Than You**

   Sorry, but sometimes their questions highlight flaws you never noticed. Instead of getting defensive, take a breath and consider: maybe their "annoying" question is the start of a better workflow.

WHY?
BECAUSE I SAID SO!

PRO TIP FOR THE OLD GUARD

Stop rolling your eyes. Instead, try: "Good question, let me explain why we do it this way." Or even better: "I don't know, let's figure it out together." You might learn something, and they'll actually respect you.

Side Note

Now, let's be real about 10% of these "Why" questions aren't coming from curiosity at all. They're coming from pure smart-ass energy, designed specifically to test your patience and have you questioning how their parents didn't murder them already. The other 90%? Genuinely curious. But when you're already on edge and your own kid (yes, the one I also work with) hits you with, "But why though?" that 10% feels more like 110%. At that point, I start fantasizing about a quick throat punch… then remember, "yep, better not."

WHINERS ARE WIENERS

Have you ever noticed how the loudest people complaining about being broke are also the ones working the least? Yeah. Spoiler alert: that's not a coincidence.

Now, before you start screaming at me in the stall while reading this, let me be clear: if you inherited money or Daddy bought you your first Mercedes, this chapter isn't about you. This is about the rest of us, the ones grinding it out.

I can't tell you how many times I've had someone whine, "I work soooo hard, but I'm still broke." No. You don't. You might think you're working hard, but let's be real, rolling into work at 9, disappearing for a two-hour lunch, and peacing out by 3 isn't "hard work." That's a part-time hobby. At that point, just admit you're running a lemonade stand for fun and stop pretending you're Elon Musk.

Here's the ugly truth: if you want money, you have to **earn it.**

That means:

- Waking up before the sun.

- Grinding until after it sets.

- Living on coffee, adrenaline, and probably some unhealthy amounts of stress.

Thinking about work when you're at work, at home, in the shower, or even while pretending to listen to your spouse's story about her coworker's cat.

Is it fun? No. Is it necessary? Yes. Is it forever? Hopefully not. The goal is to work your ass off now so later you can play golf at 2 p.m. on a Tuesday while everyone else is crying in their cubicles.

And let's not forget employees. You're not off the hook. If you roll your eyes at your boss for asking you to do your job, but you also complain that you don't make enough money, guess what? You're the problem. You want more money? Work like someone who actually deserves it.

Look, I get it, people love the phrase "work-life balance." Cute idea. But the truth is, if you want success, the balance is temporarily broken. It's more like "work-work balance with occasional pizza." Later, once you've actually made it, you can balance all you want on a yacht, with a margarita, laughing about how you used to microwave ramen.

So yeah, maybe I'm harsh. Maybe you're pissed at me right now. But here's the deal: whiners are wieners. And wieners don't win. Winners win.

Now, if you don't know what category you are in or you are in complete denial, let's cut to the chase: if you spend more time complaining than you do actually working, you're a wiener. And not even a good wiener, like a ballpark hot dog. More like a gas station roller-dog at 11 p.m., sad, lukewarm, and nobody wants it.

THE "I WORK SO HARD" CROWD

I once had an employee tell me:

"I work so hard, and I still can't get ahead."

This was the same person who:

- Showed up at 9:15 every day.

- Took a **two-hour lunch** like they were in Europe and bought lunch every day.

- Vanished by 3:45 because "traffic is bad."

Yeah, no kidding, you're broke. You worked maybe four and a half hours, and of that, it was scrolling TikTok. You don't need a raise; you need a reality check.

I HAVE TO LEAVE AT 3:45 PM BECAUSE I HURT MY THUMB!
9:15 AM
I WORK SO HARD.

THE "THERE ARE MORE THINGS IN LIFE THAN WORK" PEOPLE

Then there are the folks obsessed with "work-life balance." They clock in at 8, scroll on social media till 9, take a bathroom break at 11, lunch at noon, mental-health walk at 2, then clock out by 4 to "protect their peace."

Cool. Protect your peace all you want, but don't cry when your bank account balance is lower than your credit score. You can't Netflix-and-chill your way into success.

Work-life balance comes after years of grinding. You need your time, I get that. Hell, I do too, but I block out a certain time of the day. Mine is about 11:30 at night till I go to sleep. I call it my me time. I still eat dinner with my family and spend time with them, but I go right back to it after we are done, and they all go to their holes in the house to do their own thing. You need this time to unwind and do something to shut my brain down. That might be your gym time, reading a book, watching TV, or scrolling through TikToks. It looks different to everyone. Yes, you need this time for your sanity, believe me. The trick is to schedule it in and make sure you do it. There is a big difference between a few hours of "me" time and 20 hours a day.

ARRIVED EARLY!
8:00 AM
LEAVING LATE. WORKED TOO MUCH...
4:00 PM
5:30 PM
RELAXING AFTER ALL THAT "HARD WORK... HEH...
NETFLIX

MEANWHILE... ACTUAL HARD WORK LOOKS LIKE THIS

When I was building my business, I woke up before the sun and came home after it went down, and I still do. Almost every day, if I was lucky, I could catch up on my daily cleaning, grocery shopping, and make sure I have clean clothes so I don't smell on Sundays. Four hours of sleep. Coffee was basically my religion (which I made at home, not the $11 fancy mocha, latte chi bougie shit and if you're not a coffee person, insert energy drinks here.

And you know what? Even that wasn't enough to feel "successful." Because real success isn't built in a week. The road sucks. It takes years of grind, screw ups, late nights, and occasionally eating dinner out of a gas station bag.

So when someone tells me they're "working hard" but can't figure out why they're broke, I don't feel bad for them. I feel like handing them a mirror because they don't know what hard work is.

5:30 AM - GRIND TIME!
DINNER & CHORES... SO FUN.
MORE EMAILS. SEND HELP. #BLESSED

ENTREPRENEURS WHO SHOULDN'T BE ENTREPRENEURS

Some people start a business because they think it's a free pass to do nothing. They want to:

- Roll in whenever they feel like it.

- Take ten vacations a year.

- Treat "networking" like happy hour. If they even network

Newsflash: that's not a business, that's an expensive hobby. And hobbies don't pay the bills they cost you money. You turn your 8 to 5 into a 5 to 8 job. If you can't handle that, then your ass doesn't need to start a business. Too harsh for you, suck it up, buttercup. It is ok to just want to clock in and out and have someone else worry about the stress of being a business owner. It is not for everyone, and we need those people to work for us. You can still make a great living and actually have some type of retirement money in your back pocket.

People who tend to open businesses with fluff hours are the people who just want to pay their bills and have a little extra spending money. Well, reality check, you will not be young forever. You could get hurt, or you could get too old to physically be able to work anymore. Now what? What do you fall back on? You just spent 30-plus years working for yourself with no money in your account because you were that guy who only wanted his bills paid and never worked a little more to invest in yourself and your future. So instead of living that retirement life you are dreaming about, you will be that relative couch surfing because you can't afford to live, or that parent moving back in with your kids because "they need to take care of you now."

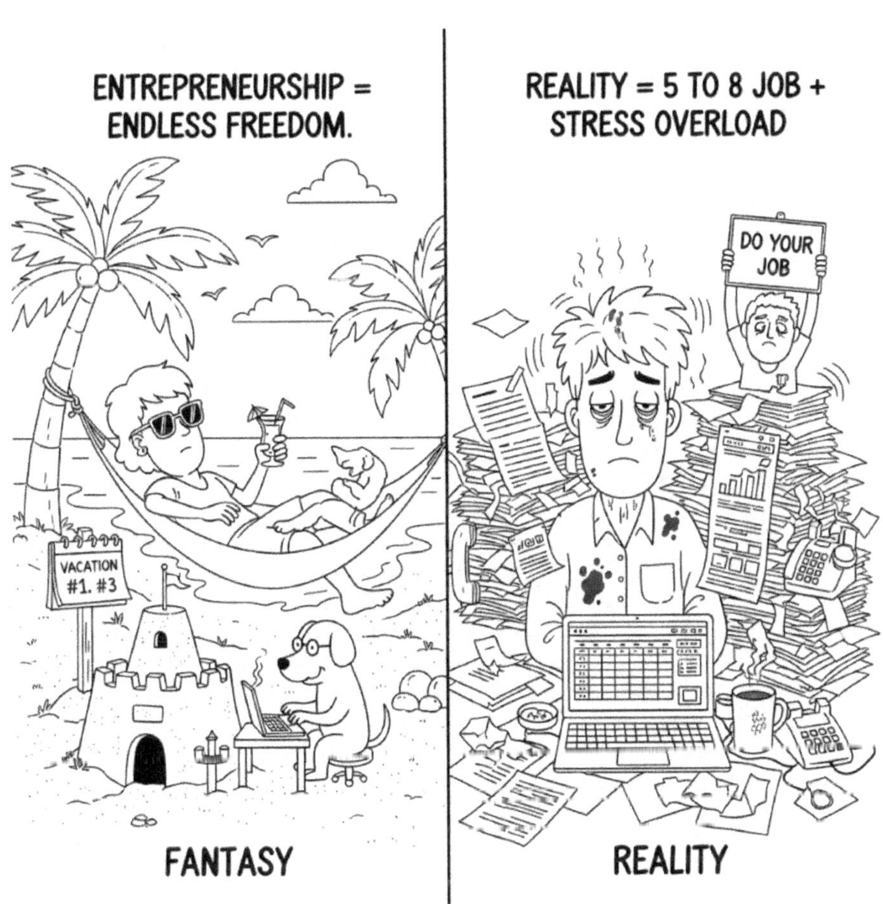

ENTREPRENEURSHIP =
ENDLESS FREEDOM.
REALITY = 5 TO 8 JOB +
STRESS OVERLOAD
DO YOUR JOB
VACATION #1. #3
FANTASY
REALITY

HERE'S THE HARSH TRUTH

If you want success, stop whining and start working. Not "pretend working." Not "I made a vision board, so I'm hustling." Actual, sweaty, boring, relentless work.

Because here's the deal:

- Whiners are wieners.

- Wieners don't win.

- Winners win. (Yes, in the real world, you do not get a "Participation trophy")

And if that felt like a Dr. Seuss poem, good. Maybe you'll remember it next time you're tempted to whine. Cheese pizza might be boring to some, but you don't complain about it when it's 3 am and you had a little too much to drink that night, do ya?

MOTIVATION PAGE:

If you're not ready to fall flat on your face, eat dirt, cry into your cereal, and then do it all again, only this time with a little more blood, sweat, and probably a bruise in a very awkward place, then this life isn't for you. You'll be so far gone that all you'll see is a tiny flicker of hope, like a firefly doing the cha-cha at the end of a very dark tunnel, and you'll have to claw, kick, scream, maybe even bite your way out just to survive.

Not ready for that? Great! Go get a safe, boring job. Work 8-to-5, sip your sad office coffee, and tell yourself you're living the dream. Meanwhile, the rest of us will be out here turning chaos into cash, laughing at our failures, and wearing our battle scars like designer jackets.

ACTIVITY BREAK TIME:

Go on your social media and post something while you're going number two. Or maybe you're doing number one. Either way, MAKE A POST.

Example:

- A photo of one of your products or services
- A before-and-after video
- photo of your work
- An accomplishment that happened today or this week
- Just be creative

BREAK TIME HELL YA

CHAPTER 5

DRUG DEALERS & STRIPPERS: THE SECRET SALES GURUS

When it comes to sales, people usually fall into one of two camps:

- The "**I was born for this**" crowd.
- The "**I'd rather eat glass than sell anything**" crowd.

But here's the truth: if you own a business, you're in sales. If you're an employee, guess what, you're in sales. And if you don't like it? Too bad. Welcome to the club. Even if you didn't sign up for it, you are in sales. Whether you're greeting customers, loading their stuff, or just standing there looking like you'd rather be anywhere else, it's still sales. You've got to smile, shake hands, and work the room like you're the damn President of the United States kissing babies. Why? Because you're not just selling a product, you're selling the company's culture. And if the culture looks like grumpy zombies? Congratulations, you just sold "misery."

Now, I'll be honest: I hate selling. It makes me feel like I'm bugging people. Why? Because I have this annoying thing called **morals**. Unfortunately, not everyone does.

But if you want to understand sales, the good, the bad, and the "damn, that's brilliant," you have to study the two best salespeople on the planet: **drug dealers and strippers.**

DRUG DEALERS ARE SALES LEGENDS

Think about it: a drug dealer doesn't run Facebook ads or hang a coupon in the Sunday paper. Nope. They know their market, they know their product is fire, and they give out **free samples.**

That's the secret. Give a little taste. Whether it's a free trial, a sample, or a discount, once someone realizes your product is actually good, they're hooked. That's not sleazy, it's smart. If drug dealers can get people addicted to garbage, you can probably get someone excited about whatever legit product or service you're offering.

STRIPPERS ARE THE ULTIMATE CLOSERS

Now let's talk about strippers. (Yes, strippers. Stay with me.)

Strippers are sales assassins because they're experts in one thing: **becoming exactly who you want them to be.** They don't sell lap dances. They sell fantasies.

- You say you're from Chicago? Guess what, they're from Chicago, too.

- Do you like football? Boom, they're suddenly a diehard fan of your team.

- You had a rough day? They get it. They're basically your therapist in heels, only they charge by the song.

And here's the kicker: a lot of guys or girls walk into a strip club swearing, "I'm not spending a dime." Yet, two songs later, they're broke, happy, and wondering how they're going to explain all the leftover singles to their other half when they do the laundry.

That's sales, baby.

SALES LESSONS FROM THE HUSTLERS

1. **Rule #1: Nobody wants what you're selling until you make them feel like they need it.**

   Addicts don't need drugs. Dudes don't need $40 for three minutes of Pour Some Sugar on Me. Yet… here we are.

2. **Rule #2: Samples are bait.**

   Free trials, free tastes, free downloads. Once they bite, they're yours. That is, if your product and services are good. If you have crap, they won't buy it (Just don't be shady about it. You're not slinging meth out of a backpack.)

3. **Rule #3: Adapt or starve.**

   Strippers don't argue with customers. They become whatever the customer wants. That doesn't mean lying; it means listening and adjusting your pitch.

4. **Rule #4: Hustlers don't apologize for the price.**

   Drug dealers don't say, "Sorry, man, I know it's expensive." They name their price and wait. Strippers don't hand out dances at the door. If people want it, they'll pay.

5. **Rule #5: Confidence sells more than product.**

   A stripper in six-inch heels has no problem walking right up and asking for your money. Meanwhile, some business owners can't even post about their product without apologizing for "bothering people." Guess who wins?

THE BOTTOM LINE

You don't have to sling dope or dance on a pole to be good at sales. But you can steal their strategies: hook people with a taste, sell confidence, and know your worth.

And if you can't do it? Guess what, hire someone who can.

There are thousands of ex-drug dealers who've turned their lives around and could outsell half the population. Or the good strippers, they already know how to work a crowd. They've got free days anyway, since nights are for college tuition… or, let's be honest, saving up for that Nissan GTR. Meanwhile, we're over here driving a $3,000 shit box and calling it "an investment in the business."

If they can sell fantasies and poison for profit, you can damn sure sell something that actually helps people. Because here's the thing: sales isn't about tricking people. It's about showing confidence, knowing your worth, and making people feel like they're getting exactly what they want, even if it's overpriced tequila in a plastic cup.

Don't lie to customers. If they don't need it, don't sell it. Your job is either to make them need it (ethically, people… calm down) or admit they don't and move on. I give customers as much info as I can, then tell them straight up: call other companies and get bids. I even tell them, "Hey, even if you don't go with us and end up with someone else, call me if they can't explain what the hell they're talking about. I'll help you anyway." You might think this is crazy, but if we are honest with ourselves, we know they will call a few other companies for more quotes.

Because here's the truth: customers don't eat, sleep, and breathe your industry like you do. Half the jargon flying out of your mouth might as well be Latin. Take the time to explain it like a normal human. I've had more customers choose us just because we treated them like they weren't idiots, even when they weren't planning on using us in the first place.

IF SUCCESS CAME OVERNIGHT, IT'D PROBABLY BE AN STD

(Ugly truth inserted) Success is not Amazon Prime. You don't get it in two days with free shipping.

Everybody loves to say, *"I want the dream car, the house, the vacation, the business."* Cool. What they forget to mention is the 3–5 years of pain, PB&Js, and sacrifice that come before it.

THE FIRST FEW YEARS ARE BRUTAL

Starting out, life is not glamorous. It's:

- Driving a beat-up vehicle that sounds like it's dying every time you start it.

- Living off ramen noodles

- Getting "creative" with social life because you can't afford happy hour. (Pro tip: water with lemon looks fancy if you squint.)

And that's not just for business owners. Employees, you're in this too. You want that dream car? The nice house? That "Instagram-worthy" vacation in Bali? Guess what, you'll need to grind for it. That means putting in extra hours, saying no to stupid impulse buys, and maybe, just maybe, not blowing $15 a day on fancy coffee that tastes like hot shit half the time because the teenager behind the counter didn't listen and made your coffee wrong. You still will drink the damn thing because you just spent 15 dollars on it.

Fancy AF.

THE MYTH OF OVERNIGHT SUCCESS

Everyone wants to believe success happens fast. Spoiler: it doesn't.

That "overnight success" story you read about? Yeah, that person was grinding for a decade while you were binging Netflix. You just noticed them when they finally popped off.

It's like planting seeds. You don't bury a seed, dump some water on it, and wake up to a tree. It takes time, effort, and patience. And sometimes, just like in business, your tree dies, and you've got to plant another damn seed.

WHY SACRIFICE MATTERS

You can't "have it all" right away. If you want more later, you have to give up some things now. That means:

- Skipping nights out.

- Driving something affordable instead of leasing a car you can't pay for.

- Learning how to stretch $50 into a week of groceries. (Shoutout to Ramen for carrying entire generations.)

Sacrifice Isn't fun. But it's necessary.

EMPLOYEES, THIS IS FOR YOU TOO

Don't think this only applies to entrepreneurs. If you're working a job and want bigger things, guess what? You still have to grind. Promotions don't fall from the sky. Raises don't just show up on your paycheck.

If you want more money, you have to bring more value. Period. That might mean staying late, taking initiative, learning skills outside your job description, or just not acting like the workplace version of a wet blanket. No one got ahead by saying, "This is not in my job description." However, there is a line to this. DO NOT GET WALKED ON. Do not be the 'yes' person all the time, because when you finally say no, you may be sorry, as you get called to HR. I learned my lesson that way. There is a happy middle ground. People get so used to you saying yes that when you finally are too busy and have to say no, they have a tantrum and report you to HR or your boss because you weren't being a "team player." Sorry, Lynn, it's been 10 years since I busted my ass in this company, been promoted numerous times, and I am the VP of Engineering now. I can't go run to the store and get you office supplies anymore."

You are not better than them, hell, if you have time or you're going out, do a solid and help them out, but do not drop everything you are doing to do it because guess what? You will be the one in trouble with your boss when your work is not done or messed up because you were too busy saying yes to everyone else.

YES!
YES!
NOT
JOB
YES!
NOT
MY JOB.
We need
to talk...
PROMOTIONS DON'T
FALL FROM THE SKY,
GENIUS.

THE 10-YEAR PAYOFF

Here's the deal:

- Grind for 5-7 years.

- Struggle. Sacrifice. Eat like a broke college kid.

- Then, in 10 years, you'll look around and realize you're living the life you once dreamed about if you actually listen

It won't happen tomorrow. But it will happen if you stop whining, stay consistent, and keep showing up.

THE BATHROOM READER REMINDER

If you take nothing else from this chapter, take this:

Success doesn't come overnight. It comes after years of nights you didn't sleep, days you didn't spend, and things you didn't buy.

So, the next time you're jealous of someone's dream car, remember you didn't see the years they spent eating Lunchables just to afford their rims. But you focus on the person who's in year one and has a new lifted truck. Because they couldn't sacrifice shit to build their dreams, they are in so much debt that they make America's debt look like your Tuesday night bar tab.

Go on TikTok if you don't have it, get it, and look for a business topic, marketing, video creation, whatever your heart desires, and hit those heart buttons. Your algorithm will show you business videos that will help you. While you're on the "break," you can get business ideas. Puppy videos are fun and all, but add some business clips to your algorithm. Place that thumbs up, like, or heart next to it and thank me later. You will learn things that no college can buy.

CHAPTER 7

COMPETITORS: THE FRENEMIES YOU SECRETLY NEED.

Here's the thing about competitors: most people see them as the enemy. Like some corporate version of The Hunger Games. "It's me or them! There can only be one!"

But in reality? Your competitors might just be your best referral partners.

THE "ENEMY" MYTH

When you're new in business, you probably look at competitors like:

- They're stealing your customers.

- They're stealing your ideas.

- They're stealing your lunch money.

Relax. The truth is, there's usually enough business to go around. And if there isn't? That's not your competitor's fault. That's your marketing problem.

WHEN COMPETITORS BECOME GOLD

Think about it:

- Maybe your competitor is too busy and can't take on more clients. Guess who they'll refer those extra people to? Someone they trust.

- Maybe your competitor doesn't do exactly what you do. Example: You detail cars. They are a mechanic shop. BOOM referral partnership. These people are in your sphere of influence.

- Maybe your competitor is great at small jobs but hates big contracts. You love big contracts. That's an alley-oop just waiting to happen

THE "COOPETITION" STRATEGY

Instead of spending your energy hating on competitors, try working with them. It's called **coopetition** (yeah, it sounds cheesy, but it works).

Here's how:

1. Build relationships. (That means talking to them like a human, not glaring across the street like you're in their rival gang.

2. Figure out where your services don't overlap and work with that.

3. Trade referrals.

4. Win together instead of crying alone.

The easiest way to find your sphere of helpers is to:

- Go online and search for them. When you are on Facebook and someone asks for a hair salon. Check out the most tagged businesses, and that is who you need to talk to.

- Go to shows, conferences, or networking events in your area that focus on your market and introduce yourself. Build a relationship with them if they aren't assholes.

- Do it the old school way, and when you are driving, stop into their place of business.

- Think outside the box: If you are in detailing, like I mentioned before, go to body shops, collision centers, dealerships, custom painters, county offices, realtors, window tint companies, and other detail shops. The possibilities are endless.

I'M NOT REFERRING ANYONE!
KAREN
?
REFERRAL
I COULD STEAL YOUR LUNCH MONEY

A FUNNY REALITY CHECK

Look, not every competitor is going to be your buddy. Some are jerks. Some will badmouth you. Some will undercut you on price like they're running a Dollar Store. That's fine. Forget them.

But the smart ones? They'll realize that:

- Referrals make everyone money.

- Collaboration saves headaches.

- And at the end of the day, no one wants to work 24/7 and still turn away customers. It is a good problem to have, but sometimes you need help.

BOTTOM LINE

Your competitor isn't always your enemy. Sometimes they're just another hustler trying to survive like you. And sometimes, they can become the person sending you more business than your marketing budget ever did.

So, ask yourself: are you wasting time hating your competitors, or are you smart enough to make them your best referral partners? For the people still shaking their heads, being stubborn, saying, "Hell no, I am not doing this." Then to you I say, " Keep your friends close and your enemies closer." I know you heard that before. That saying hasn't been around since the beginning of time for no reason.

Insert Karen's here: "I am not referring one of my customers to someone else.: Well, guess what, you just lost a lot of business. If you do and you lose your customer, guess what? Wait for it, it is going to sting. **YOU ARE DOING SOMETHING WRONG.** If you have a loyal customer and explain to them that you can't wash their dog this week, but you have someone who is amazing and can get you in, and they agree. If that customer starts using them, you are slacking. You are effing up on your customer service or your quality of service. Period. Then you need to figure out why, fix it, and move on. Or better yet, have the balls to nicely call your old customer and ask them why they left you. Most of the time, the customer will tell you.

Referrals = More Business Than Ads Ever Did.

BAD REVIEWS DON'T KILL BUSINESSES, BUT YOUR CRYBABY REACTION WILL

You know what actually makes a business look legit? Not being perfect.

If every single review you have is a shiny 5 stars with no complaints, people start side-eyeing you like, "Hmm… is this real, or is this business just paying their cousins and grandma to leave reviews?"

GOOGLE: OUR MODERN DAY BIBLE

- Need a plumber? Google it.

- Need a pink stuffed pony? Google it.

- Need life advice? Okay, maybe don't Google that, but you probably will anyway.

Let's face it: the internet runs our lives. Google is basically the modern-day Bible. You want answers, you type it in that little box.

So yes, reviews matter. They matter a lot.

In Reviews We Trust
Search: Forgive Me, Google, For I Have Sinned.
Need plumber ASAP.
Pink stuffed pony near me.
Should I text ex drunk at 2 am.
Should I text my drunk at 2 am.

THE HARSH REALITY

We all want those perfect, glowing 5-star reviews. But here's the truth:

- People are way more likely to write a bad review than a good one.

- People love drama.

- If someone has a bad experience, they'll tell their mom, their brother, their dog, AND that random stranger at the grocery store.

When was the last time you went to a store, got great service, then immediately pulled out your phone and typed, "Wow, John in aisle 7 really changed my life today?"

Exactly. You didn't. But if John pissed you off? You'd be on Google reviews before you even got back to your car.

THE SECRET WEAPON: REPLY

Here's the key to reviews, good or bad: **always reply. This is your time to shine, BABY**

- If it's good: thank them. They actually stopped their busy life to say something nice about you. Appreciate it. It's honestly more than you do right. And if you are that random person who always writes reviews. Congrats, you are that random unicorn of society, and we don't deserve you, but we appreciate you.

- If it's bad: reply anyway. That's your golden opportunity.

And when you reply, do it smart:

1. **If you were wrong:** Apologize. Thank them for pointing it out. Fix it. Boom done.

2. **If you weren't wrong:** Tell your side of the story. But do it with class.

Notice I didn't say "rip them a new one." As much as you'll want to unload, don't. Instead, use facts. Use truth. Be professional. (Basically, be the adult in the room while they're throwing a toddler tantrum online.) If you do not know how to do that, guess what. There is a little thing called AI now, where you can make your rant and ask them to type it professionally, and they will do it.

REAL LIFE EXAMPLE

We've had a couple of bad reviews ourselves. And instead of ignoring them, I wrote novels. Proof, screenshots, receipts, the whole nine yards.

Guess what? It worked. We got customers because of those reviews. People said, "We loved how you handled yourself."

Because here's the truth: there are people out there who just want something for free, or who wake up cranky and want to be that asshole to make your day bad because their life is miserable. If you respond with honesty, professionalism, and just a pinch of smart assery (yes, I made that word up)? The world sees that. And they respect it.

BOTTOM LINE

Bad reviews don't kill your business. They make you look real. They make you look human. And they give you a chance to show the world how you handle problems.

So next time someone trashes your business online, don't panic. Don't hide. Don't cry into your corner. **Reply. Own it. Tell your side.**

Because in business, how you handle the bad can actually win you the good.

THE DOLLAR STORE GUIDE TO A MARKETING GENIUS

This is the chapter where I piss off a whole bunch of marketing people. And honestly? I'm fine with it. I've got multiple degrees in marketing, amongst other things, and let me tell you, 80% of it felt like paying a lot of money to learn common sense dressed up in fancy PowerPoint slides and classrooms where everything the professors taught us was pretty much outdated 4 months later.

Now, before all you marketing folks grab your pitchforks and hashtags, hear me out. I'm not saying all marketing is free. But if you're just starting out and don't have the money to burn, or worse, you do have money but you're dumping it into the wrong places, then you need to hear this:

STOP SPENDING STUPID MONEY ON STUPID MARKETING.

Here's the real secret: **find what works for YOU**. Not what your competitor does, not what your best friend swears by, and definitely not what some "business coach" in a rented Lamborghini screams on Instagram. Find a local business coach that can help you in YOUR area if it is in your budget. Unless you want to go national, how would Randall in the Lambo know your local events, economy, neighbors, while he is at his house in LA, and you're in a small town running your manufacturing company or coffee shop?

Depending on your industry, maybe it's print ads. Maybe it's social media. Maybe it's walking into every networking event in town and shaking so many hands you feel like you just got hired as a Walmart greeter. Whatever it is, do it cheap first, then double down on what works.

And let's clear this up: free can work. Really well. But you have to track it. Every time a new customer calls, ask them, "How'd you hear about us?" (And no, the answer isn't "your mom told me to call you," though hey, referrals work too from relatives.) I mean, you can track them as well. It is always good to send thank-you emails or gifts to your biggest fans.

Do that for six months, and suddenly you'll know which of your "brilliant marketing ideas" are actually brilliant, and which ones are about as useful as paying for a billboard in the middle of a cornfield.

3 A.M.
Dog Biscuit Ads!
#CrushIt
#CrushIt
#HustleBro
LEASED
Now that's marketing!
SMITH & SON PLUMBING
SMITH & SON PLUMBING!

TOP 6 DUMB WAYS TO WASTE YOUR MARKETING DOLLARS (AND WHAT YOU CAN DO INSTEAD)

1. **Buying followers**

    Because nothing screams "trust me" like 10,000 followers and 3 likes on your post.

    ☞ **Do this instead:** Build real engagement. Post content people actually care about, tips, behind-the-scenes, funny fails, or even memes. One genuine comment beats a thousand ghost followers from who-knows-where.

2. **Putting your logo on pens**

    Congrats, your brand is now rolling around at the bottom of a stranger's purse, covered in gum wrappers.
    ☞ **Do this instead:** Put your brand where people actually use it. Coffee mugs, magnets for your fridge, phone stands, tote bags, things that don't vanish like socks in the dryer.

3. **The giant billboard in Nowhere, USA**

    Yes, Dale, I'm sure your plumbing business is going to get a huge boost from all 17 cows that pass it daily.

    ☞ **Do this instead:** Go hyper-local. Sponsor your kid's Little League team, slap your logo on their jerseys or on the fence at the field. Boom. Suddenly, every parent at the game knows your name (and probably yells it when the ump makes a bad call). Or design branded work gear and hats that are actually cool, stuff people *want* to wear out. Congrats, you've just created an army of free walking billboards. Bonus: zero cows harmed in the making of this marketing plan. ✘

4. **Radio ads at 3 a.m.**

Shoutout to all the insomniacs and long-haul truckers who now know you sell organic dog biscuits.

☞ **Do this instead:** Run ads where your actual customers are awake, on Facebook, Instagram, Google, or even a podcast they listen to. (Trust me, dog owners are not discovering you between Metallica and weather updates at 3 a.m.)

5. **Sponsoring random crap**

"Thanks to Bob's Tax Service for sponsoring this llama parade!" Yeah, that's gonna bring in clients.

☞ **Do this instead:** Sponsor events or causes that make sense for your brand. If you do taxes, maybe a finance seminar. If you sell dog biscuits, sure, sponsor the local dog adoption event, not Llamapalooza.

6. **Paying hundreds to attend seminars instead of speaking**

Why pay hundreds to sit in a room while someone else talks? You can be the star.

☞ **Do this instead:** Grab any chance to speak in front of people and tell them about yourself or your company. Free advertising, instant credibility, and bonus points for not falling asleep in the front row.

7. **Attend a conference, don't be a vendor.**

Why pay for a table at a conference when you are just starting out? Yes, you will have your promotional items and 8-foot table, but you are pinching pennies. You can't compete with the others there right now. You have to work your way up to get that fancy vendor set up. You are also locked behind that 10x10 area the whole time.

☞ **Do this instead:** Pay to be an attendee. Grab a handful of business cards and start working the conference. Go to the vendors and other attendees. You will pass more business cards out, meet more people, and network more that way than waiting for them to come to you behind your vendor booth. We have been to many conferences as events, and I will say we have had more success working the rooms than being locked behind a table all weekend.

Marketing doesn't have to drain your bank account. It's about being creative, scrappy, and actually paying attention to what works. Spend smart, test small, and laugh at the dumb stuff other people are wasting their money on.

Because let's be honest…sometimes the best marketing campaign you'll ever have is just word of mouth, telling people what you do and not being a jerk while you do it.

SOCIAL MEDIA: WE LOVE TO HATE IT, BUT DAMN IT WORKS

Here's the thing about social media: it works. But that doesn't mean you need to be on every single app that drops. Nobody has time to post on Facebook, Instagram, TikTok, Snap, Pinterest, LinkedIn, YouTube, Yelp, Twitter (or "X," whatever Elon wants us to call it this week), while also running a business, eating, sleeping, and maybe seeing your family. Unless you've got a robot or a teenager, you're not going to keep up with all of them.

The good news? You don't need to.

THE BIG QUESTION: WHO ARE YOU EVEN TALKING TO?

Before you even think about posting, ask yourself: Who is my customer? Not who you wish was your customer (like rich people in Miami buying yachts), but who actually buys from you right now.

- What age are they?
- What gender?
- Where do they live?
- Do they even own the thing you sell?
- What are their hobbies?

And just as important: how far will you actually travel to get business? If it costs you $100 in gas to drive out and make $50 in profit, congrats, you just paid to work for free. Your dream customer might love your TikTok in New York, but unless they're paying for your plane ticket and hotel, that "like" isn't buying your groceries. Unless you are selling a product, you can ship to them.

yepp
yelqp
BOOST
$$$ SNACKS
FUND
WILL
WORK
FOR
Wi-Fi
I DON'T WANT
YOUR PRODUCT,
IN THE
COMMENTS!
I DON'T WANT
YOUR PRODUCT,
BUT I WILL ARGUE
THE COMMENTS!
YELLOW
PAGES
WARNING
BLUNT WEAPON OR
PAPERWEIGHT ONLY

FACEBOOK: THE NEW YELLOW PAGES

Facebook isn't just where your aunt posts Minion memes or your mom finds out all the gossip and makes sure to tell you every detail about George's life and struggles; it's the new Yellow Pages. If you do not know what the yellow pages are, it was a magic book that weighed so much you could probably kill someone with it if you hit them. No, but seriously, it was a book that had everyone's business in YOUR area in alphabetical order by category. Believe me, it was not as fun as I am making it sound. When people need referrals, they ask Facebook. "Who knows a good plumber?" "Where should I get my haircut?" "Does anyone know who's selling a used car?"

If your business isn't on Facebook, you basically don't exist. But here's my warning: never ever click that shiny blue 'Boost Post' button. That's like mailing Mark Zuckerberg a blank check with "For Snacks" written in the memo line.

If you want ads that actually work, use Ads Manager. Just search "Ads Manager" online, and it will pop up. You get to pick how much you spend, it's simple, and it lets you target people who might actually want what you're selling instead of wasting money showing your post to a random grandma in Ohio who just wants to argue in the comments.

INSTAGRAM: PRETTY PICTURES, PLEASE

Instagram is eye candy. Nobody's there to read your novel; they're there to scroll, double-tap, and move on. Think visuals: photos, reels, graphics.

Here's a hack: connect your Instagram to your Facebook. Post once, and it shows up on both. Work smarter, not harder. You don't get extra points for logging in twice.

PINTEREST: THE SLEEPER HIT

Most people sleep on Pinterest, but it's secretly the ninja of the internet. Google loves Pinterest. If you have a good photo posted, it can rank higher on Google Images than your actual website or even Google itself.

PRO TIP

Always link your Pinterest posts back to your website. Otherwise, you're just giving people free eye candy with no way to buy or contact you. And honestly, how many times have you clicked on an image before a website? Exactly.

YOUTUBE: GREAT FOR FAME, MEH FOR RENT MONEY

YouTube is awesome if you want to be famous. Less awesome if you want to pay rent this decade. Unless you're one in a hundred million who goes viral, the ad money isn't life-changing. Plus, the way all these influencers are dropping like flies, I like my life, thank you very much. I don't need to drink that tea anytime soon.

That said, it's fantastic for "how-to" and educational content. People trust YouTube when they're learning. Just don't quit your day job expecting YouTube checks to roll in. It is a good source to get people involved, but you have to be consistent with it.

PRO TIP

If you want subscribers, make sure you are posting at the same time every week or at least have a schedule so they know when your next video is coming out. Like, every Wednesday at midnight, "The new cooking with Cathy video is coming." This helps more than you know to gain followers and traction. Especially if they look forward to your new content. I personally can't wait for every Monday because I know that the new Bailey Sarian is out. Look her up and thank me later.

YELP AND GOOGLE: THE REVIEW KINGS

- **Yelp:** Think iPhones and Apple Maps. If someone searches for a service on their iPhone, Yelp pops up.

- **Google:** The king of all reviews. If you want people to find you, you want reviews here.

Here's the secret: ask for reviews slowly. Don't go hit up your entire family reunion in one day. If you get 20 reviews in 24 hours, it looks shady, like you bribed everyone with pizza. Pace it out. Make it natural.

TIKTOK & SNAPCHAT: FUN, BUT NOT GETTING YOU YOUR RETIREMENT.

Snapchat is great if you're trying to keep your parents out of your business and want to attract a younger generation of customers. Your content disappears, and it creates FOMO. The fear of missing out. This is a good sales tactic, but not really good for most businesses. TikTok is the entertainment king. It's fun, it can go viral, and it's amazing for brand awareness. However, if you are not willing to post a lot, and I mean a lot of content, do not waste your time on the app. It is for entertainment, and if you're trying to sell that viral face cream, TikTok is the place to sell it. They didn't invent TikTok shop just because it sounded cute.

LINKEDIN: THE NOSY NEIGHBOR APP

Think of LinkedIn as the nosy neighbor for professionals. People aren't stalking your business; they're stalking you. What you're doing, what you've accomplished, what job title you gave yourself this week.

It's great for **networking, hiring, and bragging about awards**. Not as great for direct sales, but it makes you look legit. I am not saying you can't market this way. You definitely can, but most of the time, your target market isn't there to buy stuff; they are there to find out about a company, and look for a job or customer.

RANDOM BUT CRUCIAL

- Join local Facebook groups. **Gold mine.** Thank me later. That is where people go to ask for services and product recommendations. The more groups you are in, the better. However, do not go in groups, you will not provide your service or products.

- Don't ask for 50 reviews at once. You'll look desperate, and they look fake.

- Don't over-post. You only need to do it 3-5 times a week, and that is enough. If you over-post, people might start to unfollow you because of your constant sales promotions in their faces. Social media was built for entertainment first and then branched to marketing, so I don't think you want to see Jim's lawn service on your page every other post, so don't do the same to others. 3 is a safe number and easy to manage weekly to start out. Then work your way up to 5.

- Mix it up: reviews, promos, your company wins, before/after photos, videos.

- And for the love of all things holy, **reply to people**. Customers have the attention span of a gnat with Wi-Fi. If you don't answer fast, they'll hire the next guy. The biggest downfall to a business is not replying to someone. There are other businesses out there, and they will quickly move to the next. If you want to be on all these apps and have all these streams of exposure, make sure you are constantly checking your inbox. Messages, comments, tags, etc.

- If someone tags you in a post, reply back to them with a quick Thank you and then comment yourself. Introduce yourself and tell them you are private messaging them with all your information.

Save yourself the time: In your phone and on your computer, make generic responses and save them. That way, when you have to private message someone or post something, all you have to do is copy and paste it.

Bottom Line: You don't need every app. You need the right apps for your business. Focus where your customers actually are, post consistently, and engage like a human, not a robot.

Put your kids to work. Or your niece who can't stop posting bathroom selfies. Teenagers are basically cheap labor who already live online 24/7; they know the viral songs before you do and can crank out content like it's oxygen. Just give them your expectations, goals, and a general idea of your brand, then get out of the way. Let them run wild, making posts, edits, and videos. You'll be shocked at how fast it turns into actual marketing.

Don't want to babysit TikTok or Instagram? There are companies that will post and monitor all your social media at once. You hit "post" one time, and boom, it goes across every platform. If you're cheap and want to DIY it, fine. Just take a mountain of photos and video clips, then batch them. Sit down for a couple of hours, schedule everything out, and save yourself from that daily panic of, "Oh crap, I haven't posted in a week." Bonus: You can literally queue posts while sitting on the toilet. Efficiency at its finest.

I could post the top websites that do this, but technology changes every day, and what was the best today will not be tomorrow. Just Search

" Best platform to post across multiple social media sites."

Activity TIME:

At work: Post something and tag your business location; it will boost your status on Google and search engines. Do this as often as you can.

Note: You do not have to be at the location to tag it. You can be sitting in your whitey tighties or birthday suits, dancing around your house to '90s R&B. Google doesn't care what you are doing.

11

REALITY CHECK-YOUR BIGGEST CHEERLEADERS AREN'T WHO YOU THINK.

Let's get real for a second, and I am going to drop a truth bomb you probably do not want to hear. Your biggest supporters are not going to be your family and friends. Yeah, I said it.

Now, before you clutch your pearls or try to defend your best friend Steve from elementary school, let me explain myself. I hit the jackpot with my family. They are amazing. A little off the wall sometimes, (Okay, maybe a lot), but still the kind of people who had our back when we said, "Hey, I'm quitting my job with amazing pay and benefits to start over. I am going to gamble our life savings on building a business from scratch." Instead of calling me insane, they raised their pom-poms and shouted "GO TEAM."

But here is the kicker: as much as they love me, they're not the ones going to be handing me my millions. They will be the ones to support and love me, and maybe bring me a casserole when we are broke that week, but they will not be paying my electric bill.

The HARSH Truth about Friends.

You're going to have two sets of friends in this entrepreneurial circus you call your work life. It is like high school all over again with different cliques.

SET ONE: THE OLD CREW

They are the friends you've had since way back. The ones who know the embarrassing stuff about you, like that time you threw up in a Taco Bell drive-thru or cried because your boyfriend or girlfriend just dumped you because they were assholes. They're the ones who will now get mad at you because you can't show up for every birthday party, weekend getaway, or Tuesday night happy hour. And some of them… well, let's just say jealousy is a nasty green monster. They'll roll their eyes at your success while pretending to be supportive.

Some of these friends bitch because they have no money, but are the first people to never be at work, complain about their jobs like they aren't the problem, or have big dreams and no action. They're the life of the party. When you go out with them, the conversation is all about gossip, who's dating who, who gained weight, what's trending on TMZ, and of course, why Taylor Swift is or isn't ruining football. These friends are your "escape from hell" crew. They're your reset button. You laugh, you gossip, you drink too much, and for a few hours, you forget that you maxed out your credit card buying business stuff.

But here's the thing, you're not going to grow from these conversations. They're fun, but you don't leave dinner thinking, "Wow, I just got a new strategy for scaling my business!" You leave thinking, "Wow, I probably shouldn't have eaten that third basket of mozzarella sticks."

Fun for the night, but no new business strategy gained.

SET TWO: THE NEW CREW (AKA BUSINESS PEOPLE DISGUISED AS FRIENDS).

Then you've got the people you meet through business customers, clients, networking events, those random folks you hit it off with at a conference because you both made fun of the same PowerPoint slide, or how Mr. Thompson was picking his nose the whole presentation.

These people? They're golden. Because when you hang out with them, you still laugh your ass off, but the conversation hits different. They're talking about which CPA saved them thousands, which marketing strategy actually worked, and they're tossing ideas around like they're playing entrepreneurial dodgeball.

You'll learn more from a two-hour dinner with these people than from any business book. Including this one. (Yeah, I said it.) Because these people get it. They are in the trenches with you. They are speaking from experience, not theory. Their focus is growth, not gossip. They are not jealous of your success; they want you to win, and they will help you do it free of charge.

THE MIDDLE GROUND

Now listen, I'm not saying you should dump your old friends like last week's leftovers. (Although, let's be honest, some of them you should've cut off years ago. You just don't have the balls or the energy to do it. You know exactly who I'm talking about. Yes, that friend. The one who "forgets their wallet" every single time the check comes. They're basically a financial leech disguised as a drinking buddy.) You still need those wild nights where you drink too much, sing bad karaoke, and forget about work for five minutes. They're your break from the grind.

But you also need to recognize the shift. Your "fun time" friends are good for laughs. Your "business time" friends are good for building your empire. And if you're smart, you'll balance both without feeling guilty, but honestly, I don't personally feel guilty for creating my dream.

Because here's the deal: the old crew gives you memories, but the new crew can help you get millions and also give you memories.

Side Note: How do you know when you're changing? Simple: When your old crew is talking about Stacey's thirst traps online, you will blurt out, "Did you guys see the new marketing trend on Facebook?" Or when someone complains about being broke, and instead of being sympathetic towards them, you think, " Maybe stop buying those $5 energy drinks three times a day, Ronald, and save your money.?

The reality is you need both sets of friends. The old crew to give yourself the break you need once every three months, and the new crew to keep you motivated, accountable, and remind you why you are killing yourself in the first place. They challenge you, push you, and drag you up when all you want to do is lie face down in the Target parking lot.

BALANCING FUN AND EMPIRE LIKE A PRO.

12

STOP ASKING FOR ADVICE IF YOU DON'T WANT TO HEAR IT

This one's going to sting a little. Consider it less of a "chapter" and more of a vent session with educational value. I could make a whole hustle podcast about this. This one really pisses me off.

Here's the deal: I've learned my old crew of friends doesn't ask me for advice anymore. Why? Because I'm too honest. Apparently, people don't like it when you give them the truth without sugarcoating it. But here's my philosophy: why even call yourself a friend if you're just going to lie?

Now, don't get me wrong. I'm not saying you should roast your best friend for wearing an outfit that looks like it would be something their 14-year-old daughter would wear. That's cruel. I'm not a monster. What I would say is, "That's a really nice outfit. I wouldn't wear it, but it's a nice outfit." See? Honesty. Still supportive. Nobody cries in the bathroom. It was a cute outfit, just not on them.

But let's talk business, because the same principle applies.

THE PAUL PROBLEM

The number one question I get from new business owners is this:

"What can I do to get customers? I'm trying everything and nothing's working."

And every time, I want to say: **No, Paul. You are NOT trying everything.**

Here's what's actually happening:

- Your hours say 8 to 5 on Google. You show up at 8:32, leave at 3:00 because "no one came in," and then cry about not having customers.

- Someone tells you networking is the single most powerful tool for building a business, and your response is, "Nah, not my scene."

- Or my personal favorite: "I can't, I have to take my kids to school."

Newsflash: you do not get to complain about not having customers when you're skipping the very things that bring them in. If that's your attitude, you don't need to be a business owner. You don't even need a promotion. You need a nap because this lifestyle is not for you. As a mother myself, you are not the only parent in the world. If millions of parents, including single parents, can do it without affecting their work, then you can not use that excuse either.

STOP WASTING PEOPLE'S TIME

And while I'm at it, stop asking people for advice if you're not going to take it. Nothing makes me crazier than when someone asks me a question, I give them the answer, and they completely ignore it. You are wasting their time when they are trying to help, when they could be focusing on their own things.

It's like when my husband asks me something, I tell him the solution, and he just stares at me like I'm speaking Greek. Then a week later, his buddy Mike says the same thing, and suddenly it's, "Wow, that's genius. Mikey's brilliant." It was like god himself came down and gave my husband the best advice in the world.

Excuse me? I just told you that a week ago. Now I'm sitting here plotting whether strangling you would hold up in court. If this becomes a New York Times bestseller, he probably still won't listen to me. Ha Ha.

This is just an example: He actually does listen a lot. But I am trying to make a point.

SELF DEFENSE?
NOT GUILTY?

THE HARSH TRUTH NOBODY TOLD YOU

If you want something, whether it's a business, a promotion, or the life you've been dreaming about, you have to live and breathe it. Point blank.

And here's where I might offend you: if you're reading this book, nodding along, and then saying to yourself, "Hell no, I'm not doing that," then guess what? You don't actually want it. You should not be a business owner.

I'm sorry for the harshness again. I'm sorry your mommy didn't tell you this growing up. But you are delusional if you think you can half-ass this and win. This isn't a hobby. It's not a "fun little side gig." It's a lifestyle change.

It sucks.

It's stressful.

It will age you five years overnight.

But in the end?

It. Is. So. Worth. It.

ACTIVITY TIME:

Ask your clients, customers, and friends for location posts. While they are at your location or office, have them "Check In." This will help with search engines.

How, you ask?

- Contact your friends and family to do location posts. Have them "check in" to your place of business even if they are not there.

- When your client/customer is checking out or picking up their items, ask them to post a photo and add your location.

- Tell your customers/clients to "check in" whenever they are at your property and give them a discount. It doesn't have to be much. A 10% off or $5.00 off purchase is well worth it.

WOMEN IN THE INDUSTRY — CHALLENGE OR POWER PLAY?

Let's get one thing straight before we dive in: this isn't one of those "power to the women, let's burn our bras and scream at the patriarchy" kind of chapters. If you came here for that, wrong book, sweetheart.

What this IS about: the hilarious, frustrating, awkward, and straight-up powerful reality of being a woman working in any industry. It's the stuff no one puts in the corporate HR training manual. (Shocker, right?)

This is about women who are working, whether you are the owner or an employee. This chapter is also for you men who sometimes don't know how to handle women, because let's be honest, people think we as women are so difficult. (Yeah, like we're out here solving quantum physics just to order dinner.) Truth is, we're actually pretty simple: feed us, don't lie to us, pick up after yourself, and maybe act like you listened when we told you the story the first time. That's it. No secret code, no Rubik's Cube, just the basics. Women constantly feel like they have to prove themselves. We then usually go home after work, and we start our other job as a partner, wife, or mom. If you are a woman in a male-dominated industry, it's fun.

Basically, you walk into a trade show and it's like playing Where's Waldo, except Waldo is wearing mascara and heels and everyone's staring at her like she's lost. And with today's world of he/she/they/cat/carrot, who even knows how those percentages shake out anymore. But the bottom line? Women are still the minority, and that's actually one of our biggest weapons. It is not a pity party of one over here. But in this chapter, we will tackle women in the industry. How can we help you, men, with some pointers inside and outside of work, so that you can relate this to an employee?

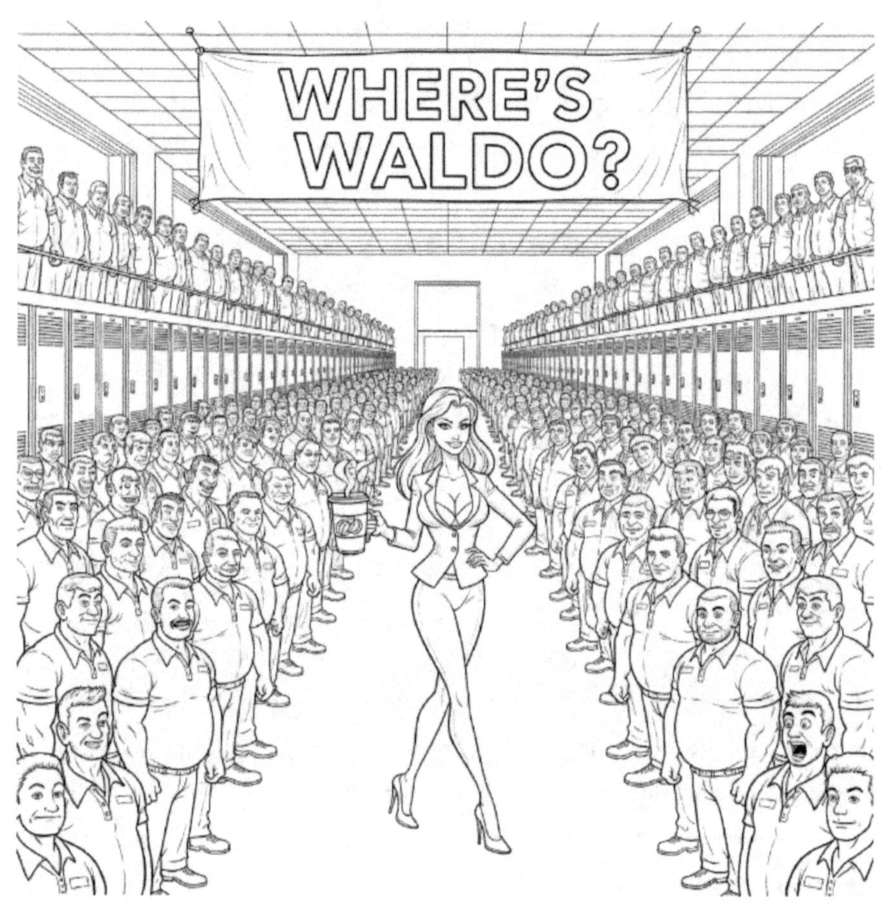

WHERE'S
WALDO?

THE SECRET OF WOMEN (NO, NOT THAT SECRET)

You want the inside scoop? It's simple: **read the personality.**

- For employees, men or women: some need a pat on the back every five minutes, or they wilt like lettuce in the sun. Others? They'd rather you leave them alone and let them work in peace.

- For bosses: newsflash, it's never just clock in, clock out. Women bosses, just like men, are grinding long after the lights are off; however, they are probably answering emails in bed while also mentally reorganizing the fridge.

LISTEN, DON'T FIX

Most women don't need your solutions, gentlemen. They don't even need your opinion. They just want to be heard. It is that simple, I promise.

When any woman in your life is venting with volume, hand gestures, and facial expressions that belong in a Broadway play, it doesn't mean she's mad at you. It means she's venting. Sometimes she can be mad, and there are THOSE people. I can say this, I am a woman LOL, but don't tell them that.

How do you handle it, you ask? What do you do? Nod. Say: "Wow, I'm sorry you had to deal with that." That's it. That's the magic line. Unless she directly asks you for advice, keep your mouth shut. Yes, keep your mouth shut, no matter how hard it is not to. I am trying to save you.

And for the love of all things holy, **never**, ever tell a woman to calm down. If you enjoy breathing and not sleeping on the couch, just don't. That phrase is basically a button that launches World War III. Instead, try: "I hear what you're saying. Let's take a step back and figure this out." Boom. Same outcome. Zero casualties. No death on today's agenda, fellas.

Dont say it,
dont say it,
CALM DOWN!
...ANYWAY!

WHAT WOMEN DO BETTER THAN MEN (BRACE YOURSELF, GUYS)

This is where women cheer and men roll their eyes so hard they can see their own brains. But hey, truth is truth.

- **Explain things.** Women are talkers. You know it, I know it. But in business, that's gold. Customers love it when you take time to break things down. And honestly? Half the time, the men didn't explain crap because they were too busy assuming the customer already "gets it." Spoiler: they don't.

- **Attention to detail.** Have you ever had someone clean your house, and you walk in thinking, "wow, that's clean," but then your wife says, "Not MY clean." Exactly. Women see the stuff men miss. (Yes, behind the toilet counts as cleaning.)

- **Willingness to learn.** Women feel they have to prove themselves twice as much, so they're the ones studying at night, watching YouTube tutorials on their lunch break, and practicing after hours.

- **Organization.** Most women need organization, and men love the messy organization tactic. Organization is good, and it works differently for people. If you want to be really organized with everything labeled and alphabetized as a female. She will be flinging those color-coded files and pulling out that label maker from her back pocket like she is ready for a showdown.

BET. WATCH AND LEARN.

ADVANTAGES OF BEING FEMALE

1. You stand out in a sea of men. (It's like walking into a biker bar with a pink umbrella; you're noticed immediately.)

2. Other women feel comfortable with you.

3. You're forced to be more knowledgeable and confident just to prove yourself, which, guess what, makes you better, and yes, women do that.

4. Women balance both a business and service mindset, which makes clients stick.

5. We see things differently. You don't believe me, just look who picks out most of those amazing colors on the cars you drive. Women have an eye for things. Use it to your advantage and ask for advice.

DISADVANTAGES (BECAUSE WE KEEP IT REAL HERE)

*   Getting taken seriously. (Cue the client saying, "I'll wait to talk to the guy." Oh, thanks, Steve, let me just slap on a fake mustache real quick so you feel comfortable.)

*   Being labeled a bitch for speaking up instead of being "intelligent."

*   Having to prove you know your stuff over and over… and over.

*   Risk-taking: men tend to leap, women tend to measure the distance ten times over before jumping. (Sometimes good, sometimes paralyzing.) Not every woman, though. I am a do it now and ask questions later type of person. I will let you know how it is working later.

STORY TIME:

If I had a dime for every time a customer asked to "talk to a guy instead of me." And honestly, I don't mind grabbing one of the guys. But here's the best part: the crew will straight-up tell them, "I appreciate you asking me, but she knows more about this than I do. Whatever she said is probably better information than I could give you."

That right there… That's gold. Because nothing feels better than having your own team back you up, instead of just standing there in awkward silence while someone disrespects you. It's not just support, it's a middle finger wrapped in professionalism.

THE DOUBLE STANDARD GAME

Here's the truth bomb: **you can't have it both ways. Women**… Don't demand to be treated equally, then milk situations just because you're a woman. Perfect example: try to argue with everyone to be treated equally one day, and then make your boss or employees feel awkward because you can't come to work the next day because you have cramps. That is just straight bullshit, and you know it. You are purposely taking advantage because if they say no, god forbid, you will be the first person running to HR. Take some Advil, grab a heating pad, and get to work. Don't tell me that mine can't be that bad. I dare you to call my mom or husband now and ask them about the hell I go through every month. But guess what, I am there, on time, and ready to do my job.

Take Away: Own your spot. Speak up if something bothers you; don't assume men can read your mind. They can't. They never will. So don't get mad at them because of it.

Be confident. Use your superpowers: better communication, empathy, and organization. That combo wins customers every time.

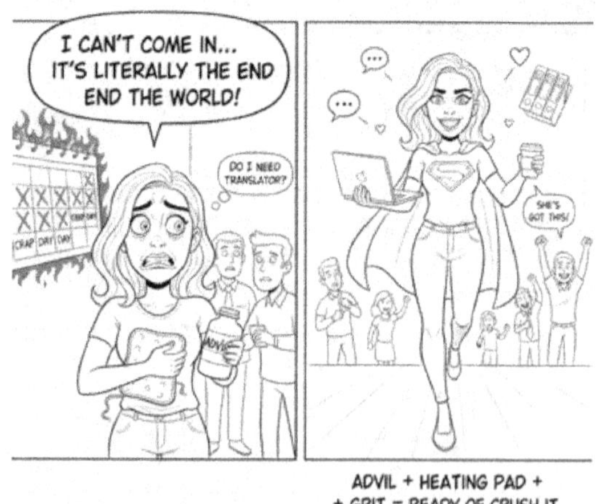

ADVIL + HEATING PAD +
+ GRIT = READY OF CRUSH IT.

The biggest issue in decision-making? Food. I have never argued with a guy about what I want to eat… and you're laughing, I know, but it's the truth. It always starts the same way: "Where do you want to eat?" → "I don't know." → Four hours later, you're hangry, slamming doors, and reconsidering your entire relationship.

The fix? **Rotate.** *One person picks three places, and the other chooses from those three. Next time, swap it. Simple. No screaming, no door slamming, and way less hanger. Plus, you can use this same system for literally any decision. Try it at work, try it at home, hell, try it when picking what Netflix show to binge. Decision made. Sanity saved.*

CHAPTER

14

IT'S TOTALLY OK TO BE A MAMA'S BOY

Gentlemen, let's get something straight: being a mama's boy isn't a weakness. In fact, it's probably the smartest business move you've never considered.

Think back to your childhood. When life got tough, who did you go to for advice? Dad? Maybe, but he was probably fixing something with duct tape or cutting the grass. Grandma? Nah, she was busy knitting or yelling at your dog. Mom. That's right. Your mom.

Why? Because moms listen. They care. They protect. They don't tell you to suck it up and "man up" (well, most of the time. They might sneak that in when deserved). They hear your problem, they process it, and they give you a perspective you never even knew you needed. And guess what? You survived. And probably thrived.

So why not apply the same strategy in your professional life? Women in your company, your wife, girlfriend, employees, clients, or mentors have the same instincts. They listen. They protect. They notice things you might miss. I might go head-to-head with the guys I work with, but guess what? I am the first person who goes toe to toe with someone who goes after them. It is that mama bear syndrome that we do. Our job is to protect.

Need a second opinion on a big decision? Ask a woman. Want insight on how to approach a client? Ask a woman. Need someone to see the tiny detail that will either make or break the deal? Ask a woman.

This isn't about hierarchy, it's strategy. It's about using all the tools in your toolbox, and the women around you are some of your sharpest, most underutilized tools.

And bonus: just like Mom, they're not afraid to tell you the hard truth… in the kindest, most brutally effective way possible. Which, honestly, is more useful than a hundred "Yes-men" any day.

So, embrace it. Be a proud mama's boy professionally. Your business (and sanity) will thank you.

FINAL THOUGHTS

Men, women, whatever box you check, nobody's "the best" in your industry. There's always someone better. Be humble, keep learning, network, and for crying out loud, support each other.

And ladies, remember this: You cannot have it both ways, and being the only woman in the room isn't a disadvantage. It's your **power play.** Because, like it or not, every single guy in there noticed you the second you walked in. Use it. Own it. Make it work for you.

WHAT THE HELL DO I POST WITHOUT LOOKING LIKE MY NEIGHBOR KEN? HE IS AN ASSHOLE, BTW

This one right here is probably the most common question I get from business owners about social media.

"What the hell should I post?"

My answer? It depends. (And yes, I know that answer makes you want to throat punch me, but stick with me here.)

Here's the deal: content is not one-size-fits-all. Your business is different. Your audience is different. Hell, even your grandma is different. (Mine is posting constant conspiracy theories, and yours might be swearing that AOL is going to make a comeback.)

So, before you even THINK about posting, ask yourself: Who am I trying to reach?

- Are they sweet little old ladies who knit sweaters for their cats?

- Are they busy professionals who have zero time and pay for things because "time is money"? (Like detailing their car. Nobody needs that, but everyone wants it because they don't want stale fries and dog hair stuck in their cupholders.)

- Or maybe it's the widower down the street who just wants someone to show up, do the job, and not rip them off.

Once you know WHO you're talking to, you can figure out WHERE they hang out. (And no, TikTok is not where your ideal manufacturing client is scrolling after a long day on the forklift. Don't even try it.) I mean, they could, but they are not looking for business connections. They are there to see that person eating it face-first because they tripped. They want to laugh and relax after a long day.

Grandma finds businesses in the church bulletin or from a flyer on her fridge. Millennials check Instagram because they trust some random influencer with too white teeth. Your corporate client? LinkedIn or business groups on Facebook. Or maybe they only respond when their HOA newsletter tells them to call. The point is you have to know where your people are hiding out..

BUT WHAT DO I POST?

I'm so glad you asked. Here are some ideas you can steal:

1. **Behind-the-scenes.** People are nosy. Show them how the sausage is made (figuratively, unless you literally make sausage).

2. **Client stories.** Share testimonials or before/after shots. Proof beats promises every time.

3. **Quick tips.** Give people little nuggets of wisdom that show you know your stuff. Your sharing is not going to make Shannon want to change her own tire, so don't think you're giving away any secrets that are going to your grave.

4. **Culture posts.** Remember, your business is more than the service; it's the vibe. Share your team, your story, your WHY.

5. **Seasonal stuff.** Tie into holidays, community events, or even stupid trends if it fits. (But if you're a law firm, maybe skip the TikTok dance challenge. Nobody wants to see you floss in a dress suit, unless you are fully tatted with a six pack.) Then you are going to get a whole different type of clients. You're welcome!

ANYTHING BUT THIS...
FOR SALE

THE GOLDEN RULE:

And for the love of everything holy, TRACK IT. I've said this before, and I'll keep drilling it into your heads until it sticks like the lyrics to that random grade school song you have zero business still remembering. (Don't lie, you know every word, complete with hand motions.) When new customers call, ask them how they found you. Write it down. Six months later, look at the data. Did Facebook posts bring people in? Did that print ad flop? Did your cousin's "viral" video get you zero leads but a lot of pity likes? Good. Now you know what works and what's just wasting time. So don't waste your time and money on it.

Content isn't about posting for the sake of posting. It's about connecting with the right people, in the right way, in the right place.

So next time you're panicking about what to post, remember:

- Know your audience.
- Find where they hang out.
- Keep it fresh.
- Track what works.

And most importantly… don't overthink it. Sometimes, the dumbest posts get the biggest traction. (Trust me, I once posted about tripping and falling on the floor at our shop and got more engagement than an ad I paid $200 for. Go figure.)

TOP 5 DUMB CONTENT IDEAS THAT ACTUALLY WORK

1. **The Office Dog.**

    Post a picture of your dog lying on the floor. That dog will get more likes than your entire marketing campaign. People will know your dog's name before they know your company name. We even dress him up in our company sweatshirts. Now, he looks at us like we are dumb humans, but it works.

2. **Random National Holidays.**

    "Happy National Donut Day!" (even if you sell accounting services). Doesn't matter. People will eat it up literally.

3. **Memes.**

    One good meme about Monday mornings will outperform your polished, professionally shot video every single time. People don't want perfect; they want relatable.

4. **The Oops Post.**

    Spilled coffee on your paperwork? Printer jammed again? Congratulations, you now have a post. People love knowing you're human.

5. **Food Pics.**

    Doesn't matter what industry you're in, post a picture of tacos and suddenly everyone is paying attention. Bonus points if you tie it to your brand: "We'll work on your taxes if you bring us tacos."

NATIONAL DONUT DAY:
BOW DOWN TO
THE REAL KING!
I'M STILL WHOLE ON THE INSIDE

Here's another pro tip: don't get lazy with your content. Switch it up. Run a promo. Highlight a different service. Change your messaging so people don't scroll past your posts thinking, "Oh, it's the same crap again."

Think of it like dating. You wouldn't wear the same shirt to every date (and if you would, we need to have a whole other conversation). You have to keep it fresh, keep it interesting

YOU DON'T NEED A DEGREE TO BE SUCCESSFUL

Okay, buckle up, because this one might make some get their panties in a bunch. Parents, professors, and guidance counselors everywhere are probably going to light a candle vigil after reading this, but somebody has to say it:

You do **not** need a degree to be successful.

There. I said it. And guess what? It's true.

In fact, in the real world, street smarts will kick book smarts in the ass ten times over. Sure, your professor with the elbow patches might have a lot of theories about business strategy, but meanwhile, Bob from the bar figured out how to flip pallets on Marketplace and is out here making six figures without ever writing a thesis paper.

Let's rewind, shall we? Remember being a kid? You wanted to be a cowboy, a ballerina, maybe even Batman. Then you hit high school and suddenly every adult in your life expected you to know exactly what you wanted to do for the next 60 years while you're still trying to figure out how to work a washing machine, why your face looks like it's auditioning to be a slice at Domino's, and how deodorant is apparently optional for half your classmates.". Spoiler alert: **you can't know.**

Unless you were that rare breed who came out of the womb screaming, "Scalpel, please!" and went straight into being a brain surgeon, chances are your career path has looked more like a drunk man falling down a flight of stairs. Messy, painful, but somehow you end up at the bottom, going, "Well… I'm still alive, so let's try this again."

Now, let me give it to you straight: I have multiple degrees. Fancy, right? Guess what else I've got? More student debt than it costs to build a custom house… with a pool, a three-car garage, and a butler named Jeeves. And you know what I learned? Two things:

1.   I learned way more about business from actually working with people than I ever did sitting in a classroom.

2.   My husband, who dropped out of college, is sitting in the exact same position as me, except he doesn't owe Uncle Sam a penny. So, who's the genius now? (Yeah. That one still stings.)

If you figured out your passion early, congrats, you overachieving unicorn. The rest of us have probably changed careers 7 times since high school. Half of us are in jobs we didn't even know existed back when we were forced to pick a major. "Digital marketing strategist"? That wasn't a thing in 1999. And others are in careers, massaging people's asses for a living. Have you seen that viral video of a guy doing that for a living? That was hilarious. That kid was all upset it wasn't at career day.

And before you roll your eyes, remember some of the most successful people in the world didn't even bother with a degree. (Insert your favorite "college dropout billionaire" here. They're everywhere. It's practically a club at this point.)

The truth? You can learn literally anything you want without dropping $50k a semester. Online courses, YouTube, networking, shadowing people, getting your hands dirty, or just straight up asking successful people, "Hey, how'd you do that?" I just saved you thousands of dollars, see? This book has already paid for itself. You're welcome.

WHO NEEDS A DEGREE WHEN YOU GOT HUSTLE

GRADUATED AND EVERYTHING I LEARNED OUTDATED
STUDENT LOAN DEBT
STUDENT LOAN BILLS
STUDENT LOAN
STUDENT LOAN BILLS
TUICION
DEBT

HERE'S HOW YOU PLAY IT SMART:

- Want to start a trucking company? Don't take out $80k in loans. Go work for a company that trains you, pays for your CDL, and basically lets you get paid to learn. Then take all that knowledge and flip it into your own business.

- Want to be a badass hairstylist? Go get licensed that will cost you some money unless your lucky to get a scholarship, then intern at a salon that does free ongoing training. Hit up conventions. Learn trends. Do hair until your hands cramp, and open your own chain of salons. You'll get farther than someone who just waved around a cosmetology diploma.

And here's the kicker: I'd rather hire someone with **zero experience** than a fresh graduate who won't shut up about how "that's not what we learned in school." Guess what, Jim? I don't care what your professor said. At my company, we don't follow the sacred "Principles of Business Management 101." We follow the "How to Actually Make Money and Not Cry at Night" handbook. Big difference.

The best part, if you hit the ground running during High school or as soon as you graduate, you are now a minimum of four years ahead of all your old classmates. While they are just graduating from college, getting an entry-level position, you could be the person who is actually interviewing them because you are ahead of the game.

Fun Fact: People always tended to look down on the blue-collar workers/trades. Tattoo artists, welders, powder coaters, and construction workers, just to name a few. Guess what, half of them are making over $50-$150 an hour minimum, depending on their experience, because no one wants to get their hands dirty anymore.

CHAPTER 17

BUSINESS PARTNERS –AKA FREE THERAPY OR FREE BANKRUPTCY

If you want my opinion (and you obviously do since you're still reading this), my answer is simple: **HELL. NO.** Run. Sprint. Fake your own death if you have to. Do whatever it takes. Because I have never, and I mean never, seen a business partnership work out the way people think it will.

Let me clarify: yes, partnerships can work out. I've seen a few that are wildly successful. But the percentage? Not great.

Have you ever heard of Ronald Wayne or Steve Wozniak?

…Yeah, didn't think so, but maybe you have.

Wozniak was the actual mastermind behind the Apple I and Apple II computers. Nine years in, he bailed because he didn't like where the company was headed, and yet Apple is still cutting him checks to this day. A round of applause for Wozniak, but I don't think Apple is happy about it.

Now Wayne? That poor guy lasted 11 days. He thought Apple was too financially risky, so he tapped out and sold his 10% stake for wait for it; $800. If he had kept it, those same shares would be worth over $100 billion. Bet he's still kicking himself square in the ass every morning.

Here's the problem: You need two human beings with the exact same plan, dream, drive, caffeine addiction, and level of insanity to make it work. That's basically like finding a 1998 Toyota Twin Turbo Supra in a barn with 0 miles and window stickers on it still. Rare. Impossible. And even if you do find one, give it time; it'll blow up in your face eventually.

Now… full confession: I do have a business partner. Shocker, right? It's my husband. (Pause for dramatic gasps.)

Yes, I know some people escape their spouses by going to work. Me? I thought, "Hey, why not just add QuickBooks to the list of things we can fight about instead of leaving the facial hairs from shaving just after I cleaned the bathroom?" I know you know what I am talking about.

Yet somehow, we make it work. But let's be clear: that's not advice. That's a miracle. The fact that we haven't ended up on a true crime documentary yet is proof there's a God. I think it's because he hasn't found a way to get rid of my body without getting caught.

WHY DID I THINK
THIS WOULD BE
EASY.
BUSINESS
PARTNERSHIP:
WHAT COULD
POSSIBLY GO
WRONG
FUN
FUND

BUT... HERE'S THE TWIST

There are circumstances where a partnership can actually work.

Like if you somehow find that one mythical creature who's willing to work 7 days a week, 16 hours a day, fueled by the same delusional dream you have. That's rare, but it exists. (I married mine. Pray for us.)

Or maybe you're not looking for a "ride or die" co-captain, but more like a sidekick with money. That's when you bring in an angel investor, a silent partner, or someone who basically says, "Here's a pile of cash, I believe in you, now don't call me unless my check bounces." And honestly? That can work beautifully. Sometimes we all need a little help, and there's nothing wrong with that. However, there are always those pesky strings that are attached.

But here's the deal:

If you do it, if you decide to bring anyone into your business, get a lawyer.

Not some free AI-generated template you found on Google at 2 a.m. I'm talking about a full-blown, airtight contract. The business prenup, per se. Pay for it now so you don't pay triple when it all goes to hell later.

Because I promise you: it always sounds amazing at first.

You're sipping beers, brainstorming business names, picking fonts for your logo, and then one day your "best friend" empties the bank account because they suddenly discovered meth is more fun than payroll.

Yep. That happened in one of my husband's previous business adventures. I can't even make this shit up, honestly.

So, yes, sometimes a business partner can work out. Sometimes it's your spouse. Sometimes it's an investor. Sometimes it's a unicorn in human form. But more often than not, business partners are either:

- Free therapy, or

- Free bankruptcy.

PRO TIP:

If you can, save up enough cash to cover 6–12 months of your personal bills before you even think about diving headfirst into business. That cushion will save your sanity when the slow months hit.

Then, buy your equipment, software, and tools gradually. Piece by piece. Do it yourself where you can. Rome wasn't built in a day, and neither will your company be. So quit stressing about having it all at once. Build smart, not broke.

Just remember, choose wisely.

CHAPTER 18

BUSINESS PAGE VS. PERSONAL PAGE — AKA "HR IS STALKING YOU LIKE THE FBI"

Decide early: **Are you going to have a business page, a personal page, or both?** And if both, which one is going to be the place where you accidentally ruin your career?

Here's the thing: I wasn't my own boss my whole life. Nope, I had bosses, HR, corporate policies, and Ben from accounting breathing down my neck like they were in charge of the FBI's Most Wanted list. I swear, I got sent to HR more times than Diddy has had accusations. (And that's saying something.)

Was it my fault? Well... yes and no. Let me explain.

Back in the day, I was a VP at a management company (fancy title, still broke), and one day, the President of Sales reported me to HR because of something on my Facebook page. But here's the kicker, it wasn't even MY post. It was my MOM.

What horrible, offensive, fire-me-immediately thing did she post? A picture of a shirtless dude with a six-pack, dressed as Santa, holding a puppy with the caption: **"Merry Christmas from your Secret Santa."**

That's it. That was the scandal. Not a bong rip. Not a pyramid scheme. Not even a passive-aggressive meme about my boss. A dude. With abs. Wearing red velvet. Holding a dog.

I honestly, admit it, you wish your mom were that fun. I know I got lucky. (But trust me, that's a whole other book.)

Anyway, to this day, I still think that was the dumbest thing to get in trouble for. Like, seriously? That was my personal page. I couldn't control what my mom posted! What did they want me to do, ground her? Change the WIFI password?

I mean, yeah, I could've just set my page to private or deleted the post. But come on. It wasn't like I was posting, "Here's my block of weed, can't wait to get lit tonight, wish me luck on the P and L statements tomorrow!"

(Side note: I legit had an ex-employee do that once. Kids these days… bless their dumb little hearts.)

THE POINT: PEOPLE ARE NOSY AF

Here's the reality: people are nosy as crap. Everyone magically turns into a private investigator the second they want to learn more about you. I swear, give me your first name and a blurry selfie, and I can find your ex's ex's dog's Instagram, your kindergarten report card, and your grandma's blood type by dinner time because everyone wants to share EVERYTHING online.

So, trust me when I say this: **Don't post anything online that you wouldn't want your boss, your customers, or your nosy Aunt Debra to see.**

Because the employee/coworker who doesn't like you? They're your #1 fan online. They're camped out with popcorn, waiting for you to slip up. And those customers you're trying to impress? They're digging through your Facebook photos like archaeologists, trying to "get to know you."

Me? I've got both a business page and a personal page, but honestly, they mirror each other. All work, a little bit of personal, nothing incriminating. I let people relate to me without giving them ammo to take me down, but since my life is all work, I will say my scandalous dream evening is getting home before 8:30 pm and having my pajamas on by 9:00 pm on a good night.

We will dive deeper into this topic later.

KEY THINGS YOUR BOSS, CUSTOMERS, AND CO-WORKERS DO NOT NEED TO SEE:

- You smashed off your ass at a bar doing karaoke to "Baby Got Back."

- Your family drama. (Nobody needs a Facebook Live of you fighting with your cousin over the gravy at Thanksgiving.)

- Your 3 a.m. political rants in ALL CAPS.

- Your thirst traps. (Unless you're a fitness influencer. Then go off, King/Queen.)

- Your "side hustle" that's actually just an MLM selling bedazzled cat collars. Make a different page for that.

- Screenshots of arguments in your DMs, stop giving people free entertainment.

- How much you love your partner. Ohhh Jennifer, we saw that meme you posted yesterday about how you feel all alone. Relax, you do not need to convince us that your love story is deeper than Romeo and Juliet. We know you are lying. He is a piece of crap, and if you forget how that ended… spoiler, they both died.

- The breakup. The girls post thirst traps with too many filters. The guys only post pictures of their kids, and prior to you didn't even know they had any. Yes, girl, you are in your 40s, acting like a 20-year-old. You are so cool. Yes, Bobby, you love your kids all of a sudden, and you're the best father in the world we know. Insert massive eye roll here. WE don't care.

!WHOOPIE!
!*#@*!
SING IT!
FLAOOMES

IF YOU HAVE TO POST THAT WILD STUFF (AND LET'S BE REAL, SOME OF YOU CAN'T HELP YOURSELVES), THEN:

1. Make a completely separate, locked-down page for only your closest friends and family. I know this will be hard because you need that validation and the sympathy from people.

2. Or… just keep your personal pages completely private.

3. But also remember, nothing is ever truly private online. Once it's out there, it's out there. Forever. (Somewhere in a server farm in Utah, Mark Zuckerberg is laughing.) Thank God I never got a phone call about my son's private parts. Because 15 years from now, can you imagine the headline? "Future CEO of Powder Coating Empire Makes Bold Market Move… and Also Forgot Pants Are Optional." Shareholders confused, LinkedIn in chaos, TED Talks canceled, and somewhere, a life coach is screaming, "This is why we teach them hygiene and boundaries!" Meanwhile, I'm in the corner sipping beer like, "Yep, that's my kid… always thinking outside the pants."

Moral of the story: Business page = professional. Personal page = fine, but keep it safe. And if your mom posts Santa thirst traps, just pray HR has a sense of humor.

Easy on the filters, champ. If you smooth your face so much that you look like a wax statue, don't be surprised when people are shocked to meet the real you. Half of you out here catfishing, and newsflash, your man looks better as a "pretty girl" in those filters than you do half the time.

CHAPTER

19

SAVE YOUR MONEY, IT'S NOT ROCKET SCIENCE

Alright, listen up. Whether you're an employee grinding toward that dream car or an entrepreneur trying to join the ranks of us gloriously insane business people, saving money is not hard. I repeat: NOT HARD. If your favorite actor lived in their car, showering at friends' houses before they hit it big, you can survive a few microwaved meals and a slightly less fabulous lifestyle. Let's face it, running a business is expensive, and even if you're not trying to be a business mogul but just an employee with dreams of getting that house. Most of us don't have a secret vault of gold coins we dive into every night like Scrooge McDuck. But you can save money without looking like you're eating Spam… every night.

HERE'S HOW:

Don't eat out like you're auditioning to be a food blogger.

Do the math. Add up all your DoorDash, Uber Eats, Taco Bell runs, and nights out hitting the $12 margarita special. Just pull up last month's bank statement and get to adding. You'll want to vomit just thinking about it. Instead:

- Be creative. Eat at home before you go out. Pretend you're Gordon Ramsay but without the yelling.

- Buy microwave meals and bring your lunch to work. You'll save $20 a day and only slightly lose your soul.

- Become your own barista. Those fancy $6 coffees I talk so much about? They are your mortal enemy. Make them at home like a caffeinated wizard. Bonus: You can name them whatever you want. "Caffeinated Crack in a Cup" has a nice ring to it.

PURGE LIKE A CRAZY PERSON BUT STRATEGICALLY.

Yes, yes, I know. I'm a massive car enthusiast. My garage looks like a car museum run by a slightly unhinged curator because we buy shit boxes and say we will fix them one day. But when we started our business, I had to make tough choices. I sold the one car that had car payments to save money, kept the essentials, and downgraded to a 2001 beater Acura Integra. It smelled funny, paint was crap, and the AC didn't always work; in Florida, no less… but we were investing in our future empire.

Sometimes you have to look at your stuff and say, "Do I love this thing, or do I love the future I'm building?" Hint: the future usually wins, but yes, it feels like stabbing your heart with a rusty wrench.

This is the part people hate hearing, but it's the truth. If you want that life where your dream car is parked in your driveway, your business is thriving, or you're the president of the company you paid your dues at, you have to live off some stale bread for a while… You have to make choices. It's like dieting, but instead of losing weight, you're gaining financial freedom.

- Want to go out every Friday night? Sacrifice it once in a while.

- Want the latest iPhone? Sacrifice it and remind yourself Steve Jobs never texted from an iPhone 17.

- Want to complain? Fine. But then go sacrifice something real.

PRO TIP

Saving money isn't about never having fun. It's about trading short-term Instagram-worthy thrills for long-term, life-of-your-dreams thrills. You can have both… eventually. Just maybe not simultaneously while still eating cereal for lunch.

PRO TIP

TIPS OF SAVING MONEY ADD UP: YOU DON'T HAVE TO CUT THEM ALL OUT, BUT EVEN SOME WILL WORK.

Monthly "Why Am I Spending This?" List

1. **Coffee Runs:** $3–5 per cup × 20 workdays = $60–$100

   (Or just make it at home and feel like a financial genius.)

2. **Takeout / Fast Food / Uber Eats:** $10–15 per meal × 15–20 days = $150–$300

   (Because cooking is apparently "too hard" after a 9-hour workday.)

3. **Streaming Subscriptions:** Netflix, Hulu, Disney+, Spotify… $10–$20 each = $40–$80

   (Do you even watch half of these? No. But hey, variety.)

4. **Gym Memberships:** $30–$100

   (Bonus: pays for access to a treadmill you use twice before you stopped going.)

5. **Impulse Shopping / Online Orders:** $50–$200

   (That $30 gadget looked important at 2 a.m. on Amazon… now it's collecting dust.)

6. **Fancy Lattes / Energy Drinks / Smoothies:** $3–$10 per drink × 10–15 days = $30–$150

   (Because caffeine is life… and apparently, an investment.)

7. **In-App Purchases / Mobile Games:** $10–$50

   (Congrats, you just bought a new hat for your virtual character.)

8.   **Brand Clothes / Accessories:** $50–$300

(Sometimes it's "for work." Sometimes it's "I saw it on Instagram.")

9.   **Snacks / Candy / Convenience Store Junk:** $20–$60

(The "I'll just grab one" tax.)

10.   **Random Monthly Fees:** $5–$30

(That one app, that membership, that trial you forgot to cancel…)

11.   **Overpriced bottled water:** $3-$5

(You do realize water is free, right? And don't be that person who is grossed out by faucet water; billions of people have survived on it, companies just made you think it is bad for you all of a sudden to make money.

12.   **Hair/Beauty treatments:** $50-450

(Do your hair at your house yourself, or just don't go as often as you normally do. You still need to look presentable, but those $1000 Botox treatments every two months are not going to kill you if you skip one time.) If you are reading this, thinking there is no way I am giving my Botox up at all. That means you probably have what we call Botox blindness.

13.   **Home services:** lawn/pool, etc $30-$300

(You can do it yourself for free on the weekends or when you get home from work; it will not kill you, and, shocker, a lot of people do it)

14.   **Monthly subscription boxes:** $20-$100

(Do you even look at them anymore, or just forget to keep cancelling it every month?)

15. **Events/Concerts** $60-$500

(Repeat after me, you do not need to drop $2000 to see Taylor Swift in the nosebleed section, especially when it will be a Netflix special in a few months)

💡 **Total Potential Waste:** Easily $400–$2500+ per month

(Imagine redirecting even half of that into your business, ka-ching!)

TRUST FALL TIME:

Don't forget those reviews: Get into a routine of asking your customers for reviews at checkout. You can even create a QR Code that they can scan right there. Tell the customer. "Would you mind leaving a Google review? It helps our customers find us better when they are online."

How to create a free QR code: Websites like Vistaprint do it for free.

CHAMPAGNE DREAMS, TAP WATER BUDGET

Let me get this out of the way: one of the biggest lies people will tell you is that you need a ton of money to start a business. Total crap unless you are starting a full-blown manufacturing company from scratch.

Now, sure, rolling up in a $100k lifted truck wrapped with your logo looks cooler than pulling into a job site with a beat-up Ford Ranger and a crooked magnet stuck to the door. But unless you've got a magic money fairy handing out zero-interest cash (spoiler: you don't), don't do it.

Here's where the real advice comes in: talk to business owners. The ones who actually started from the bottom, not the ones flashing shiny machines and brand-new signs on Instagram. We had to get creative, stretch every dollar, and figure out what was worth spending on and what wasn't.

Most new owners love to argue about this because they think fancy = legit. And yeah, shiny equipment and big signs look nice, but guess what? Being in massive debt and then realizing you should have never started the company because it's too hard is worse. You just took a massive leap, starting a business, don't bury yourself deeper with bills you can't afford.

Think outside the box, start small, and keep your stress level below "crying hysterically on the floor of your shower at night." You can absolutely look good, stand out, and build something solid without blowing a mountain of cash.

CHAMPAGNE DREAMS / NEWBIE FANTASY

TAP WATER BUDGET / REALITY CHECK

Here are some ways to launch without draining your bank account:

1.   Don't hire people when you can do it yourself

Starting a business isn't as complicated as some people make it sound. You just need to figure out the basics in your state licenses, insurance, registrations, and maybe a specialty license if your industry requires it.

Take Florida, for example: all you have to do is hop on Sunbiz, grab a name, Google "get an EIN number," and boom, you're officially a business owner. It's not rocket science.

I know every state and country is different, but here's the point: look it up, figure it out, and do it yourself. You'll save thousands of dollars by skipping the "middlemen" who want to charge you for things you can literally do from your couch while binge-watching your favorite show. All you have to do is do your research first.

2. **What Do You Need?**

Start this list early and slowly buy things. You don't need to quit your job on Friday and open your business on Monday if you don't have to. Pre-plan. Take a few months or even a few years and bargain shop for what you need.

You don't need the best stuff. You need the stuff that gets the job done. That $300 stapler? Pass. That $1.25 one from the Dollar Store? Perfect. Save the fancy gear for when your business is paying for it, not when you're maxing out a credit card just to look impressive.

3.   **DIY Marketing (AKA Be Your Own Meme Lord)**

Who needs expensive marketing agencies when there are free apps and you can AI your cat riding a tiny vacuum to advertise your cleaning business? Social media loves absurd, funny stuff. Bonus: your marketing budget goes from $500 to $5… which is basically free if you find quarters in your couch. I am not saying not to get a marketing agency eventually, just not in the beginning. Go online and use the tools to learn for free.

4.   Barter is your friend

Need a website? Trade a car wash. Need accounting? Trade that sweatshirt you're selling online. People love free stuff. You'll probably get someone to do something you didn't even know needed doing, and hey, it's cheaper than hiring someone who expects to be paid. You can also do it the other way. Maybe someone wants to hire you or buy your product, but they offer a service you need. Ask them to barter. "Hey Joey, I know you want to buy my product, but how about you help me? I will give you my product if you can post a review about it, and help me with my QuickBooks. I can't figure this out."

5. **Learn From YouTube and TikTok**

Yes, TikTok is not just for dancing teenagers. There are entire communities dedicated to how to start a business, how to negotiate, and even how to survive a zombie apocalypse (hey, you never know). Watching these videos is free, educational, and you can laugh at people falling over while they teach you something. Make sure you hit that heart button and see more pop up on your FOR YOU page so they are easier to find.

6. **You do not have to buy new?**

   Facebook Marketplace. Even though I love to hate that damn thing, I use it all the time. Do you know how many times I forget to check Marketplace? I have equipment at our shop that I am making payments on instead of buying something slightly used because someone thought that they were going to be the best business owner, and realized that they were not cut out for the grind of it, and it was too hard. Poor babies. But guess what, their loss is your gain.

7. **Network for Free**

   Those networking groups love to charge good money to join, but here's the secret: they usually let visitors in for free because they're hoping you'll sign up. Use that. Get your face out there.

   Some groups have small monthly dues (less than what you spend on that vape), and others cost more, but visiting is usually free. Hit as many as you can, figure out which ones actually work for you, and save your money for the one worth joining.

   Remember: networking is all about showing up and being consistent. Be repetitive, be visible, and you'll be memorable, kind of like that one jingle you can't get out of your head.

8. **Bigger is not always better. In some cases, anyway.**

   That shiny newer $80k dump truck looks nice, but you don't need it. You want it; there is a difference. Learn to drive a truck and trailer, and start with a beater. It'll save you a ton of money and give you more options.

   A used truck and trailer can do just about everything you need. Clean it up, maybe wrap it if you can afford it, and you've just saved yourself about $60k and made your vehicle a driving billboard. Plus, it's multi-use: unhook the trailer on weekends, run errands, and live like a normal human. Hook it back up during the week, and boom, you're making money.

And here's the kicker: if your dump truck breaks, your whole business is parked until it's fixed. But with a cheaper truck and a trailer? Worst case, you hook that trailer to something else and keep working. Flexibility > debt.

9. **Business Cards: A Thing of the Past**

I still carry business cards and hand them out, but let's be honest, most people lose them, toss them, or never look at them again. If you do want cards, don't overpay. Use a free Canva account to design one, then upload it to a site like Vistaprint. They're always running sales (40% off or more), and yeah, while supporting local print shops is great, sometimes saving money matters more, especially when you're just starting out.

Want to skip cards altogether? Make a digital business card instead. It's free and easy to set up. Just know they get lost too. Ever go to a trade show and scan 15 people's digital cards, then realize later they're buried somewhere in your phone? Exactly.

Final Thoughts:

I could probably gather all my business friends, throw a few drinks on the table, and we'd laugh all night swapping stories about how we pinched pennies to keep our companies alive. The truth is, you've got to be resourceful and creative. Honestly, I could probably write an entire book just on the ridiculous ways people waste money when starting out.

Stop being so hard-headed, thinking you "need" things you really don't. This especially goes out to all the Snap-on mechanics out there walking around with a toolbox so expensive their great-grandkids are going to be making payments on it. Meanwhile, the rest of us are out here fixing problems with duct tape, a prayer, and a Harbor Freight coupon just fine.

DON'T HAVE TIME? THAT'S CUTE.

Oh, you don't have time? Sweetie, grab a chair because we need to have a little reality check… and maybe a drink or a pint of ice cream. Or three. I'm about to school you in a master class in why "I don't have time" is the most expensive lie you tell yourself every day.

Let's be real: "I don't have time" is the adult version of "the dog ate my homework." It's cute. It's sad. And it's completely, 100% wrong. You're scrolling TikTok, binge-watching some influencer open a mystery box for 47 minutes, and somehow telling yourself you're too busy to work on your dreams? Honey, dreams don't work unless you do.

Here's a test: If your best friend called right now and said, "Pack a bag, private jet to Vegas, all expenses paid, magic llamas at the show," your ass would be in that jet faster than you could say, "Are snacks included on the flight?" And yet, somehow, you "don't have time" for your own business, your own growth, your own life? Yeah… I see you lying.

Stop lying to yourself. You've got exactly the same 24 hours as every billionaire, every CEO, and every influencer posting photos in Bali while their assistant handles their emails. Even the guy in your office who posts passive-aggressive Slack messages at 11 p.m. is dedicated enough to make time.

Let's get real. That 4-hour "I'm working, I'm too busy" block? Let me guess:

- 1 hour arguing with strangers online about whether pineapple belongs on pizza.

- 45 minutes doom-scrolling Instagram.

- 230 minutes pretending your video game rank is critical to world peace.

- 15 minutes yelling at your cat for walking on your keyboard.

- The rest? Napping like a sloth on Ambien.

And then you wonder why you're broke.

And don't give me the "I have kids" line. Oh, you have kids? So does literally everyone else in the world. Single parents? Working parents? Moms who run multi-million dollar businesses out of their garages? They make time. You are literally just bad at math, because if the world's biggest pop star can release three albums, launch a clothing line, perform at Coachella, AND give birth to twins with no nanny, you can certainly make 30 minutes of real progress today.

Now here is the kicker. Stop pretending your life is too hard. You are doing it yourself. "Pity Party of One." Your reservation is available. Figure out where your time is disappearing, hint: it's probably on some dumb, useless app where birds are doing gymnastics and actually do something. You want it, you work for it. Or… go ahead, keep "not having time" and enjoy your life as a spectator to everyone else's main character energy.

Simple steps to start:

Step 1: Identify your time thieves. Spoiler alert: it's usually you, your phone, your couch, and that weird obsession you have with watching carpet cleaning tutorials.

Step 2: Kill them. Or, you know, just limit them. Your TikTok account doesn't need you watching every single lip-sync challenge. It's not impressive. However, use it to your advantage and find some business-related inspirational videos.

Step 3: Do something. Anything. Preferably something that moves you forward. Your business doesn't care that your houseplants are thriving. Neither does your bank account.

And if you need a friend to call you out for being lazy or someone to yell at you while handing you a metaphorical boot to your ass, congratulations: you just hired me.

NETWORKING THE LEGAL WAY TO COLLECT PEOPLE WITHOUT STALKING

Networking. That magical land where people pretend they like each other just long enough to exchange business cards, but every now and then, you strike gold. You find that one group that actually has your back and wants to see you succeed. Shocker, right?

But let's be real. If you've ever gone to a networking event and stood in the corner hugging your drink like it's your emotional support animal… congratulations, you're doing it wrong.

1\. **Stop Thinking Networking Is Optional**

News flash: it's not.

If you think your business will grow just because you've got a great location, fancy banners, and an expensive sign, welcome to the unemployment line. "My name is Gina. How can I help you?"

And before you whine about the 7 a.m. breakfast meeting, guess what? Nobody else in that room is thrilled about waking up at the ass crack of dawn either. Networking isn't about schmoozing; it's about planting seeds, making connections, getting knowledge, and being remembered, and if you get lucky, you get some decent coffee and bacon.

2. **Going Once Isn't Enough**

Ever been handed a business card and tossed it in the trash before you even left the event? Yeah, same. That's exactly what happens when you put in the effort of a sloth.

Networking is about repetition. Who will you remember:

- The person you saw once, maybe twice at a monthly mixer?

- Or the person you chat with every week, who actually takes time to ask about your life?

Exactly.

3.   **It's Not Speed Dating**

Listen carefully: showing up, shoving your cards into people's hands, and sprinting out like your ass is on fire is not networking. It's called being annoying.

Work the room. Take your time. Learn people's names. Remember their dog's name. (Yes, even if their dog is named something ridiculous like "Sir Snuffles the III.") Show interest in them, and they'll take interest in you.

4.   **People Only Refer People They Like and Trust**

Would you refer your best customer to someone you don't trust? No, because you don't want that disaster blowing back on you. Guess what? Other people feel the same.

Be the person who always has "a guy."

- Need a plumber? I got a guy.

- Need a contractor to build your in-law suite far enough away that you forget they exist? I got a guy.

- Need a mechanic who won't screw you over? Yep, I got a guy.

If you're the go-to connector, people will always call you. And while you're on the phone? Boom, you sell them one of your services, too. Double win.

5. **The Art of Talking to Strangers (Without Being Creepy)**

Networking is like slow-motion speed dating minus the awkward make-out.

- **Ask questions first.** People love talking about themselves.

- **Actually listen.** That means phone away, eye contact on.

- **Use the ammo they give you.** They'll drop little nuggets you can build off of.

- **Add value.** Don't just fling a card at them and hope. Share a tip, a connection, a piece of advice, make yourself memorable.

- **Use that stripper sales mentality I talked about.**

6.   Follow-Up ≠ Dating Rules

This isn't dating. You don't have to wait three days. Follow up the same day or the next with a quick message, and bonus points if you remember their kids' or grandkids' names. People love that personal touch. I do recommend the next day because they are probably doing what you will be doing. They will be catching up with all their work, phone calls, and emails because they were at an event that day. So you don't want your email to go to the waste side.

PRO TIP

Fridays and Mondays are not the greatest days to send emails. You still can send them, but for most people (not us, obviously), Fridays are the lazy days of the week for people. They have already mentally checked out, so you might notice that you don't have people responding to you quickly on Fridays. Monday is the catch-up day. They are catching up on all their ignored Friday emails, plus their Saturday and Sunday emails. Monday, they will be deleting everything that doesn't look urgent or that they don't recognize the person's name. Again, you definitely can email people these days, you just might want to put in your head that if you don't hear from them to maybe follow up.

Keys to Networking Like a Savage

1. **Stop relying on random meet-and-greets.** Join your Chamber, industry associations, and get active online.

2. **Don't ignore the quiet ones**. The shy person in the corner might just be your first $10,000 client.

3. **Premature pitching.** (Get your mind out of the gutter.) Nobody wants a 5-minute business vomit the second you shake hands. Ease in. Small talk exists for a reason.

4. **Be memorable, not insane.** Humor = good. Too many tequila shots = bad. Stand out for the right reasons.

5. **Help first.** Give advice, share referrals, and connect people. The more you give, the more you'll get.

6. **Get involved in your community!**

Final Word

Networking isn't scary. It's that itch you don't want to get rid of. It's not optional, so if you're skipping it, good luck keeping your business alive. Done right, you'll become the most popular kid in town, that everyone knows, trusts, and calls first.

Networking will give you friends, business ideas, advice, and confidence. Hate public speaking? That'll fade fast when you're the go-to person everyone looks for.

Be the Networking Yoda: wise, resourceful, unforgettable.

PRO TIP

Did you email someone, and they never responded? That is so freaking annoying, I know. Email them back a few days or a week later with your original email and add, " Mr. Charles. My name is Gina. We met at the networking event, and I sent you an email last week. My email tends to go to spam, so I was just making sure you received it." See what I did just there.

HOW TO BUILD A KICK ASS COMPANY CULTURE (THAT DOESN'T SUCK)

(A.K.A. THE INVISIBLE CIRCUS YOU ACCIDENTALLY SIGNED UP FOR)

Have you ever worked somewhere and thought, "Wow, this place really blows." The people suck, the mission statement is just corporate fanfiction, and nobody, including the CEO, follows it? Yeah, me too. More times than I'd like to admit.

Here's the thing: no company is perfect. But the bigger they get, the faster they lose whatever personality (a.k.a. "culture") they started with. And culture is everything.

So, what the hell is business culture?

I'm glad you asked, hypothetical person.

It's the unwritten rulebook of "how we do shit around here."

It's not the handbook HR gives you (nobody reads that anyway) or the mission statement framed in the lobby. Culture is the vibe. It's the glue holding the circus together or the thing that makes you want to fake your death and move to an unmarked location.

Culture is made up of:

- **Values** → what people claim they care about.

- **Behavior** → what they actually do when nobody's watching.

- **Norms** → the sacred traditions, like who cuts the turkey at the company holiday party, or who gets blamed when the Wi-Fi goes down.

- **Attitude** → Do you show up like it's a party every day, or like you're at your grandma's funeral?

Culture is the company's personality; it's the bread and butter if you will. Ignore it, and congratulations, you're now running a business where your employees have résumés updated on Indeed before lunch break. Nurture it, and you might actually have a team that doesn't fake being sick just because they despise being in the same building as you.

MISSION STATEMENT
Q3
I knew working here would hard, but this spot?
GOOD LUCK
GOOD LUCK

So, your company has a culture, or at least a vague idea that it's supposed to have one. Awesome. But here's the secret: a culture that's all boring values on a wall and endless mandatory training sessions is about as fun as a root canal. The trick? Keep it funny, entertaining, and sarcastic without burning the place down. Here's how:

1. **Define Your Core Values... for Real This Time**

    Stop with vague crap like "We value excellence." Nobody knows what that means. Try: "We respond to customers within 24 hours or we owe them pizza. "Make sure everyone actually knows the values, yes, even that guy who only shows up for the free snacks.

2. **Hire for Culture Fit (and Tolerable Weirdness)**

    Skills can be taught. Attitude cannot. Find people who get your vibe but not clones. A little chaos is healthy; complete chaos is, well… HR nightmares. Let people show personality: quirky desk decorations, creative Slack emojis, or themed dress-up days. Normal is boring. Weird is memorable. And when weird is celebrated, culture becomes something people actually look forward to. If this is a little too much too soon, start with Friday being jean day in your office. Baby steps.

3. **Talk About It, A Lot**

    Culture is like a plant: if you don't water it, it dies. Talk, celebrate, rant, whatever, just don't ghost your team. Bonus points if you can do it without using corporate buzzwords that make people barf.

4. **Lead by Example**

    If you're yelling at the office plant while sipping your latte, don't be surprised when everyone else loses their minds too.

Your team copies you. So, model behavior you actually want to see.

5. **Accountability, Baby**

Culture dies when no one takes responsibility. Own mistakes. Apologize. Fix it. Repeat. Otherwise, you'll end up with a workplace full of passive-aggressive email ninjas.

6. **Adapt Without Becoming a Dumpster Fire**

Companies grow. Culture should grow too, just not into some bloated, meaningless corporate nightmare. Keep what works, trash what doesn't.

7. **Empower Your Team**

Give them freedom. Make them feel like mini-CEOs of their projects. If they fail, laugh, learn, and move on. If they succeed… throw a small party. We learned about the people who like the pats on the back.

8. **Sarcasm is your secret weapon.**

Sarcasm keeps people awake. It keeps them engaged. It's basically cultural caffeine. Use it wisely: funny emails, witty messages, or even a "mission statement" that acknowledges no one reads mission statements. But never let sarcasm be cruel; it's supposed to bond, not burn bridges. Yet don't be dumb, there is a line between being sarcastic and being a professional. Learn that line and use it.

9. **Make rituals entertaining.**

Rituals are cultural glue. The trick is to make them fun. Holiday parties, Friday wrap-ups, or chili cookoffs. Add a twist: costume contests, sarcastic awards ("Best Excuse for Missing a Deadline"), or random mini-games. Suddenly, culture is something people look forward to. Think of The

Office and the Duffy Awards. Michael Scott was not only a good leader but could laugh at himself.

In short, a funny, entertaining, sarcastic culture isn't about being a clown; it's about making people actually want to be there, while keeping the circus from literally collapsing. And honestly? If your culture makes people laugh at least once a day, you're already doing better than most companies out there.

TRUST FALL TIME:

From any device, go to Google Maps and enter your business address. Allow the GPS to take you to your location. This will also help move up your ranking on search engines. Do this as often as you can.

HOW TO BUILD (AND NOT COMPLETELY SCREW UP) CULTURE

1. DECIDE WHAT SUCKED ABOUT YOUR OLD JOBS AND DO THE OPPOSITE.

Boom. Chapter done. Goodbye.

…Okay, fine, I'll elaborate. When we started our company, we literally wrote down everything we hated about previous jobs and flipped it on its head. That was our playbook.

Everyone's culture will look different, but here are some of ours:

1.   **Bosses vs. Leaders**

We hated working for asshole bosses. You know the type, the guy barking orders like he's auditioning for The Devil Wears Prada, the one who tells you; you have to go to work on your day off because he wants to go to a football game. The person who forgot what it was like to get their hands dirty. If you quit, his whole company would collapse like a Jenga tower.

Solution: Be a leader, not a boss. Get your hands dirty again. It might do you some good and make you a little more humble. (Refer to the "How Not to Be an Asshole Boss" chapter for details.)

2. **Coworkers You Can Actually Stand.**

Nothing kills morale faster than working with people you'd never voluntarily sit next to at the lunch table.

Solution: We added a second interview round where future employees meet the actual crew they'll work with. If the team says, "hell no, this guy's annoying," guess what? No hire. If you're going to spend 40+ hours a week together, you'd better at least tolerate each other's breathing. You might think we are crazy because we are leaving it in the hands of our employees, but they help us build the company and make the money, so yes, they do have a say, and we are ok with that. It's worked so far, and we have very low turnover.

3. **Leave Your Baggage at the Door**

Yes, life is messy. No, we don't care that you and your pet fish fought last night.

Solution: Drop your personal shit 10 feet outside the shop. Pick it back up when you leave. If you can't? Congrats, you just won yourself an unpaid day off with Netflix and your tears. It's not harsh; it's protecting the company's Happy Bubble. Don't be the asshole who ruins everyone's day.

4.   "The Customer Is Always Right"… LOL, No.

This is corporate gaslighting at its finest.

Solution: Customers are right until they're not. We bend over backwards to fix problems, but if Karen still isn't happy after we've done everything humanly possible, we close ranks and back our team. We're a team, and teams don't throw each other under the bus unless it's Thanksgiving dinner, then all bets are off.

5. Grown Adults Having Toddler Meltdowns

Employees throwing tantrums like 5-year-olds is a rite of passage for every company.

Solution: We created the "Monthly Bitch Fest." Yup, it's exactly what it sounds like. Once a month, the entire crew can vent about anything, including the bosses, and everyone has to sit there and take it.

But here's the catch: if Jim calls out his employee for being on Facebook all day, then that said employee also gets to call out Jim for taking 20 smoke breaks. Fair's fair. It's brutal, it's honest, and weirdly enough, it works. Because after everyone vents and throws out what is bothering them, they work on it and fix it. It is not rocket science. It is called communication. And guess what, that is the key to any business.

Bottom line: Business culture is either the thing that makes people excited to show up or the reason they're quietly applying at Starbucks during lunch. You get to decide which circus you're running.

THE CULTURE SURVIVAL GUIDE

(HOW TO SPOT WHEN YOUR WORKPLACE IS ACTUALLY A DUMPSTER FIRE IN DISGUISE)

So, you're trying to figure out if your company's culture is solid or if it's secretly a cult with dental insurance. Lucky for you, I've put together some red flags to watch out for.

⚐ Red Flag #1: *"We're Like a Family Here"*

Translation: *We will exploit you, underpay you, and emotionally manipulate you, but hey, there's cake in the break room!* Families fight at Christmas and make passive-aggressive comments on New Year's. Do you really want that at work? Didn't think so.

What good culture looks like: A team that respects you, communicates, and doesn't treat PTO like asking for parole. It is not wrong to say you are like family, but no matter how perfect your family is, drama and fights come along with it. So, fight respectfully, get it over with, and move on. Think of the saying, "Don't go to bed angry."

⚑ Red Flag #2: The Mission Statement Nobody Knows

If you ask 10 employees what the company's mission is and get 12 different answers, congrats, you don't have a culture, you have corporate karaoke.

What good culture looks like: People actually *living* the values, not just walking by a plaque in the lobby that says *"Integrity, Synergy, Excellence"* (which sounds more like a law firm for evil supervillains anyway).

⚑ Red Flag #3: Bosses Who Lead Like Dictators

If you think "motivation" = yelling louder, congrats, you're in a toxic circus. You are the same clown who thinks fear = productivity. Spoiler: it doesn't.

What good culture looks like: Leaders who roll up their sleeves, actually know what your employees' job involves, and don't act like royalty on the shop floor. You will work alongside them when the time is needed.

If your office vibe makes a funeral look like Coachella, run. A workplace without laughter is basically a prison sentence with benefits.

What good culture looks like: People joking around, celebrating wins, and occasionally roasting each other in ways HR *probably* wouldn't approve of. (But hey, nobody's crying in the bathroom, so we're good.)

⚑ Red Flag #5: "Work-Life Balance" = A Lie

If you call your employees at 10:30 PM and say, "Just a quick thing," congratulations, you're making them date their job now. Hope you like spending a lot of money on recruitment.

What good culture looks like: Leaders respecting that your employees have a life and are human, not a robot plugged in 24/7. Work gets done *during work*. Radical, right? Just because you signed up for the hectic life of an owner or boss doesn't mean they did. Find a balance. If you need them like that, pay them accordingly.

⚑ Red Flag #6: No Accountability (a.k.a. The Blame Olympics)

When something goes wrong and everyone suddenly becomes a detective pointing fingers, you're not at work, you're in an episode of *Law & Order: HR Unit*.

What good culture looks like: People owning their mistakes without being roasted alive, and a team that fixes problems instead of playing Hot Potato with blame. Don't scream or yell. We all know things happen. Even BIG things. You don't get anywhere by playing the blame game. Tell everyone to stop pointing fingers and figure out how to fix it.

PRO TIP

Customers can handle screw-ups if you serve it with a side of confidence. Just say, "Yep, we hit a snag, but here's how we're fixing it and the whole team's on it." If they're still steaming, you toss out an apology and maybe even a discount. That's what the Miscellaneous Expenses line on a P&L is really for; it's not "miscellaneous," it's "sorry money." We don't like dipping into it, but hey, if a discount keeps them from chewing your ass out and even telling people that your company did great even with a hiccup, it's a win.

♟ The Culture Litmus Test

Here's the test: On Sunday night, when you think about going to work, do you…

- Shrug, maybe roll your eyes a little, but you know you'll laugh with the crew and it'll be fine.

- Feel like you've been drafted into *The Hunger Games* and start Googling "how to fake your own death."

If it's B, congrats, you've got a culture problem. Yes, we all want to be on a boat fishing instead, but unfortunately, we all have those damn things called bills and ridiculous things called dreams.

☞ Business culture is either the invisible safety net that makes people stay, or the invisible choke chain that makes them bolt. Your job is to know the difference and build the kind of circus where people want to show up, not one where they're plotting their escape.

26

EMPLOYEE TANTRUM POLICY (ETP)

BECAUSE APPARENTLY THIS NEEDS TO EXIST

Welcome to the Employee Tantrum Policy, created because some of people still think throwing adult-sized hissy fits is an acceptable way to behave at work. Spoiler alert: it's not. This will either hit home with you, and you will get offended, or this will help you deal with that pesky adult child.

SECTION 1: DEFINITION OF A TANTRUM

For legal and comedy purposes, a "tantrum" includes but is not limited to:

- Slamming doors like you're in a high school breakup.

- Throwing tools, clipboards, or any object that could double as a weapon in Mario Kart.

- Huffing, puffing, and storming out like the Big Bad Wolf.

- Crying louder than the machine shop fans.

- Being the office gossip bitching to anyone who has ears.

- Peeling out of the parking lot like your Civic just got cast in Fast & Furious 12: The Unemployed Drift.

SECTION 2: WARNING SYSTEM

If it were me, I would have no warning system, but I will make one for you just in case you tolerate these adult children.

- **First Offense:** You get a juice box and a coloring book. Enjoy your "cool down" period.

- **Second Offense:** HR (adult babysitter) sends you a pacifier in your work mailbox, if not a bag of rhino shit from an anonymous sender. (yes, you can actually do this. Google it.) Also writes you up for your tantrum, with one more warning allowed. You are officially in time-out with no pay for the rest of the day.

- **Third Offense:** Your official job title changes to "Chief Crybaby ." Congratulations, it comes with zero pay and unlimited PTO because you're no longer employed.

SECTION 3: ACCEPTABLE ALTERNATIVES TO TANTRUMS

Instead of making the workplace feel like daycare, consider:

- Taking a walk (preferably not toward your car with squealing tires).

- Screaming into a pillow (not your coworker's lunch).

- Writing your feelings in a diary (we recommend glitter pens for maximum effect). If this is your thing.

- Using your big kid words like the rest of us. In a normal, acceptable volume.

SECTION 4: COMPANY CULTURE REMINDER

This company thrives on teamwork, respect, and a shared love of sarcasm. If you act like a toddler, we will treat you like one. This includes, but is not limited to:

- Mandatory nap time.

- Getting strapped into a car seat for the ride home.

- Time-out in the corner with a hat that says, "I threw a tantrum today." (We have done this, but we have a WWE belt, we call it the Bitch Belt. You think I'm joking… I'm not.) As the owner, I will say I have worn it a time or two myself. As soon as my COO handed it to me. I laughed and wore it proudly because I did, in fact, deserve it.

SECTION 5: FINAL NOTE

If you can't handle adulting without stomping your feet, congrats, you just earned yourself a full-time promotion to home. Your new coworkers: Netflix, DoorDash, and your mom asking why you keep making dumb life choices.

Tip: This would be amazing to print out and stick in the breakroom.

THE SPECIES OF EMPLOYEES (AND WHY YOU CAN'T TREAT THEM ALL LIKE CLONES)

Welcome to the wild jungle of your workplace. Here, employees aren't just people; they're an entire ecosystem of weird behaviors, mysterious quirks, and baffling survival strategies. And if you try to treat everyone the same? Congrats. You just became the HR version of a zookeeper who forgot to feed the lions.

Let's meet some of the species you're probably already hosting:

THE OWNER (AKA THE MANIAC WITH A DREAM): IF YOU WANT TO KNOW, THIS IS ME.

- Lives, breathes, eats, and poops the business.

- Sleeps? Nah. Rest is for the dead.

- Building an empire, burns out, then makes another empire because "why not?"

- Anyone who doesn't match their grind speed looks lazy AF. Spoiler: most people don't want to live like a caffeine-fueled raccoon, and that is Okay.

LEADERS & MANAGERS (AKA BOSS JR. WITH MORE STRESS LINES):

- Got the job either because (A) they're actually competent or (B) they're friends with the owner and happened to be standing nearby when someone quit.

- Work almost as many hours as the owner.

- Note for managers and 2nd reminder in this book: Employees are NOT your 10 pm booty call. If it can wait until morning, let it wait. If it can't wait, get your ass out of bed and do it yourself. Remember: you were once the little guy, too, and they are not paid to have their Netflix time interrupted.

PAYCHECK-TO-PAYCHECK ZOMBIES (AKA "JUST HERE FOR RENT MONEY" CREW):

- Goal: Pay bills, survive, repeat.

- No interest in promotions, no overtime, no "team-building retreats."

- They will absolutely not want to do anything that is not in their job description, so don't even try to ask, and they sure as hell don't care about quarterly goals.

Pro-tip directed to the Paycheck Zombies: you cannot have it both ways. Stop acting shocked or get over your feelings when Ben, the newbie, just got a raise and you didn't. You get in 7 minutes late every day and bitch when you work 2 minutes after. He is the Company's Free Steroids see below)

CLIMBERS & OVERACHIEVERS (AKA COMPANY'S FREE STEROIDS):

- Will break their backs, crush 60-hour weeks, and smile while doing it.

- These are the people who either make your business thrive, work way more hours than they should, or, when you don't appreciate them, will take your best customers and start their own company.

- Warning: Overachievers, don't get cocky. Before you stomp in demanding a raise, maybe learn the difference between gross revenue and actual profit. You see that check got cut to the company for $10k, you don't understand that only $2k actually might go in the owner's pocket if they are really lucky.

- Just because your boss drives a "fancy" car doesn't mean they're balling. That Lexus? Paid off in 2001. That boat? Leaks. If they do have new shiny things they busted their ass for years, you didn't see, so keep walking,

- If you've got bosses who don't appreciate you (and let's be honest, plenty of them are out there), quit and find a place that does. Life's too short to work where you're miserable. But let me add the part people forget: don't quit without a plan. Make sure you've got money set aside to cover your bills, or line up another job first. Quitting without a safety net isn't brave, it's reckless.

60 HOURS?
NO PROBLEM!
CUSTOMER
SATISFACTION!!
I LOVE
DEADLINES!
PROJECT
ALPHA

Moral of the story: Employees are not one-size-fits-all. They come in all shapes, sizes, personalities, and goals. If you treat the rent-money guy like the empire-builder, he'll quit by Tuesday. If you treat the climber like a zombie, she'll start her own empire and eat yours for breakfast.

Example: Some people want to be recognized with a paper award or in the company newsletter, while others just need a "you did a great job today. Thanks for all the hard work. We appreciate you." You need to learn about them; they work for you. Try to pretend like you care if you are not that person. What do they like, what don't they like, and treat them all differently. If Joan likes that certificate and drinks Starbucks. Don't buy her a Dunkin coffee and smack her on the back for a job well done. If Jimbo gets embarrassed by an audience, don't put him center of attention. There is a fine line between being friends with your employees and their boss. But most of the time, people will be loyal to you if you appreciate them. Hell, I didn't stay at a job for 14 years because my pay was amazing. It was the benefits (I am not talking about health insurance) and how the culture was there that made me stay so long.

LEAD, DON'T MICRO-MANAGE (PUT THE MICROSCOPE DOWN, YOU WEIRDO)

First things first: If you're not an owner or manager, go ahead and skip this chapter if you want, toss it across the room, or use it as a drink coaster. This part isn't for you.

Now… dear bosses: Step. Away. From. The. Microscope.

- I know it's hard. I know your soul needs to hover like a creepy helicopter parent.

- But back it up, Michael Myers. Your employees felt your weird presence the second you walked into the room like that one horror movie scene where the villain just stands there breathing heavy while everyone pretends not to notice. Yeah, that's you.

Here's the truth bomb: There's a galaxy-sized difference between being a boss and being a leader.

- A boss = the character in every movie who storms in, wrecks the whole plot, and leaves a disaster behind.

- A leader = Gandalf. Yoda. Or hell, even Dumbledore (minus the beard lice). They guide, they teach, and they know when to get out of the damn way.

Newsflash: You hired your employees. Which means at some point, you had enough faith that they could do the job without you peeking over their shoulder like Gollum watching his "precious." So, stop breathing down their necks like you're checking if they flossed this morning.

Employees don't need you tracking their every move like you're writing a "Where's Waldo?" book about their day. They don't need you knowing what bathroom stall they used or if they double-ply or single-ply. I promise, you have way bigger shit to deal with.

If you're an actual leader, you'll:

- Teach your crew.

- Answer questions without making people feel like morons.
  - Build trust.
  - And then set those baby birds free to fly… knowing they'll soar (and maybe crap on a windshield for you).

☞ **Moral of the story:** Be a leader. Not the office poltergeist no one asked for.

MICRO-MANAGING
BOSS
TRUE LEADER
Baby Birds
Fly Here
Bathroom
Choice:
Single-Ply!

Story Time: One of our old dealerships we worked at brought in a new General Manager. And let me tell you, this woman walked in there like she was Cruella de Vil with knockoff Prada's; she tried to pass off. She was too good to talk to anyone. Had a General Sales Manager do everything except wipe her ass (and honestly, I think she would've asked if she thought she could get away with it.) She delegated everything to the GSM, cut pay, fired veterans, and made morale tank faster than a lead balloon. Meanwhile, the GSM was the heart of the place. Lived and breathed that dealership, respected the employees, took on all her dirty work (yep, even firing people around the holidays), and still managed to crank sales from 60 cars a month to 170. The place thrived because of him and the team that trusted him.

And how does her Royal Bitchness repay him? By bringing him into her office and telling him, "You are too nice to the people. If you don't start treating them like maggots under my shoe, pack your crap and get out." Maybe not those exact words, but you get my point.

And what did the General Sales Manager do? He hit her with the corporate mic drop: *"Bye, B."* and walked. We would have loved to have been there for this, but unfortunately, she decided to let our whole department go to hire her brother-in-law, so we could not witness it firsthand. That would have been so epic, honestly. But I did hear he is doing way better, and the dealership isn't selling anything, so good luck with that.

Moral of the story: Be the GSM; the one people respect, not the Wicked Witch everyone is planning your death 15 times a day.

ACTIVITY TIME:

At work: Check in if you want to be the most popular. Every chance you get, tell your crew and employees to check into the business location using your wi-fi. Don't forget about the customers, too. When you are at work, go on your phone with the wi-fi and check in with your employees and customers on Google or Facebook. This will bring your rating up on the search engine.

CHAPTER

29

PEEPING TOMS OF THE BUSINESS WORLD

Let's be real: everyone loves to act like they don't care what other people are doing, but the second someone posts a new car, vacation, or "just closed on my dream house" pic, suddenly they're a part time Sherlock Holmes, zooming in on the countertops to see if it's granite or quartz.

Here's the truth: nosy people are everywhere. Some of them are rooting for you, some are secretly hoping you trip over your own success, and some are just in it for the drama. And guess what? Sometimes it pays to give them exactly what they want, just not the truth.

THE BOTOX BUNCH: WHERE EVERY WRINKLE IS A LIE AND SO IS THEIR LIFE

There are only a few reasons to be posting about your perfect life.

Reason 1: Because you desperately seek people's approval, and you want them to think you got it all figured out. Big house, nice car, fabulous vacations every weekend… meanwhile, you're really at home every night in your sweatpants in massive debt, binge watching the latest serial killer documentary, ugly crying into a pint of ice cream.

Reason 2: You're slinging some type of pyramid scheme. Yeah, you know the ones. Where you trick, I mean "recruit" other people to sell what you are selling, overpriced shakes, lotions, or magical leggings that make your ass bigger, you make money off of them. It's basically a cult, but your posts are the bait. "Look at my amazing life!" so people will DM you asking, "OMG, how can I join?" Why, because they want to have that life you are showing them. Congratulations, you are baiting and catching them. Keep it up.

THE LITTLE TEASE

Then there are the normal-ish people. Most people fall into this category. They're like the movie trailer, not the full feature film; you get just enough to be curious, but not enough to know if you should buy popcorn.

These folks mostly post about work, but then BAM, you see a shiny new car, or maybe a random vacation photo, and suddenly you're left scratching your head like, "Wait… are they rich? Or just really good at hiding debt?"

Reason 1: They do this to make you wonder: "Are they rich? They have to be? Or did they just max out a credit card?" Either way, they want you questioning. Hell, no debt could be involved at all, but people's brains tend to lean towards Negative Nancy Vibes. Then the gossip starts.

Reason 2: They swear up and down they "don't want people in their business." Meanwhile, if you did a quick online deep dive (come on, Sherlock, you know you've done it), you'd have their kids' birthdays, their mom's maiden name, the exact date they got married, and their last three sales all mapped out. Privacy? Yeah, right.

But here's the thing: most of the time, these people are just celebrating small wins from their vision boards. And honestly? We can't even hate on them. At least they have a vision board. Some of us are still winging life with sticky notes and vibes.

Just credit card...
Just casual Friday drive...
Vacation vibes, nothing special
Big Wins
Sales charts
Kids' birthdays
Buy car
Go on vacation
Mom's maiden name

Vision boards sound cheesy, but they actually work. So bust out the scissors, glue sticks, and your inner 3rd grader, it's arts and crafts time. If you don't know what a vision board is, think science fair project meets "delusional but optimistic adulting." Slap on that Nissan Skyline, the dream house by the water, maybe a fake million-dollar check. Then hang it up, stare at it daily, and manifest the hell out of it. Worst case? You've got a collage that makes you smile. Best case? You're cruising to work in that Skyline instead of your beat-up Corolla.

THE LIVING DEAD WITH WI-FI

These are the real geniuses in the game. The ones you can't find a damn thing about online. They either run their social media from the shadows like some villain in a Marvel movie, or they've got a ghostwriter (literally) posting for them. Do you even know what they look like? Nope. These folks could walk right past you at Starbucks, and you'd have no clue because they want it that way.

They don't want anyone in their business. Shocker: they don't even have "private" accounts, because private still means Zuckerberg is watching you eat tacos. Instead, they hide everything in trusts, LLCs, or under names faker than your aunt's Facebook profile pic from 2009.

Go ahead, Google them, you'll come up empty. No flexing. No Lamborghini selfies. No "hustle harder" hashtags. They don't need it. And the kicker? If you can't find them, you sure as hell can't sue them, chase them down, or go after their assets. That's not paranoia, that's next-level boss mode. These guys have been in the game for a while, wiping people's tears with hundred-dollar bills and sneaking out like they are Batman. Why? Because they are fine with people thinking they are "normal," they have nothing to prove and don't want anyone in their business. They know that with money comes everyone trying to get a free piece of it. So, they work hard and keep to themselves because they don't have to prove anything.

Reinsurance Thought: In almost every business, there's a "Face of the Company." You know the person in every video, post, or podcast. Some people love it. Others (like me) would rather wrestle a cactus, but hey… somebody's gotta do it.

And let's be real, I can't afford to hire some ex–reality TV star to be the face of my company. So, guess what? You get me awkward pauses, bad lighting, and all. Because until we can afford that polished "professional face," small business owners are stuck being the spokesperson, the janitor, and the unpaid influencer all rolled into one, and that is ok. If not get grab that one employee or relative who loves being the center of attention.

30

YOU'RE WELCOME (FOR REAL THIS TIME)

Spoiler alert: There is no Chapter 30. That's right, 29 chapters, not 30. I know, I know… try not to have a meltdown if you're the type who alphabetizes your cereal boxes.

But hear me out: by ending at 29, I just saved you precious time, mental energy, and possibly a few brain cells. You're welcome. Seriously though. Consider this your official cure for compulsive chapter-counting OCD tendencies.

You are probably looking at me like Justice has been looking at you this whole book. Like "What the Actual Fuck!" (reference photo lol)

So go ahead, close the book, pat yourself on the back, take a deep breath, and remember: less is more. Especially when it comes to me giving you exactly what you need and nothing you don't. You survived 29 chapters. And that, my friend, is victory.

ENDING QUOTES FROM SOME OF OUR CREW:

> *"As long as your name is in someone's mouth like a Richard, you're doing something right."*
>
> **– Jason Calhoun**

> *"A glass half empty is actually half full. Stop being lazy, get off your ass, and fill it up."*
>
> **– Gina Calhoun**

> **(when something is going wrong)**
>
> *"God Bless!!!"*
>
> **– Johnathan Velez**

> **(When he thinks he knows everything)**
>
> *"I have rights, I'm basically a lawyer."*
>
> **– Taytum Calhoun**

(He swears this response goes with any question)

"Deez Nutz"

– Justice Calhoun

(For anything... just use this after everything. It's like that funny game when you were in grade school and put "in bed" after everything you say. Just use this line instead)

It's not uncommon

– Randall Reed

www.ingramcontent.com/pod-product-compliance
Lightning Source LLC
Chambersburg PA
CBHW071458140726
47997CB00005B/1771